Can't wait for the big day! *signature*

DOES ANYONE SPEAK

Female?

George & Kim,

Great to have you as our new friends. Praying God's blessings on you both!

signature

DOES ANYONE SPEAK

Female?

A guide to unlocking her heart

RON BIAGINI

TATE PUBLISHING & *Enterprises*

Published by Tate Publishing & Enterprises, LLC
127 E. Trade Center Terrace | Mustang, Oklahoma 73064 USA
1.888.361.9473 | www.tatepublishing.com

Tate Publishing is committed to excellence in the publishing industry. The company reflects the philosophy established by the founders, based on Psalm 68:11,
"The Lord gave the word and great was the company of those who published it."

Book design copyright © 2009 by Tate Publishing, LLC. All rights reserved.
Cover design by Leah LeFlore
Interior design by Lindsay B. Behrens

Published in the United States of America

ISBN: 978-1-60696-955-7
1. Religion / Christian Life / Love & Marriage
2. Religion / Christian Life / Spiritual Growth
09.05.12

DEDICATION

I dedicate this book as a gift to my three sons, Chad, Chase, and Chandler. As of this writing, they are unmarried, and their ages are twenty–two, nineteen, and seventeen respectively. *Love your women passionately. Be the world changers you were created to be. Set the bar high for others to aspire toward. You have made me so proud to be a father. Because of your greatness, people automatically think I'm great. Thank you for that honor. I love you.*

I also dedicate this book as a gift to my two daughters, Rachelle and Cheyenne. As of this writing Rachelle, age twenty–four, is married, and Cheyenne is fifteen years old. Let this serve as an aid to my current and future sons–in–law so they have a marriage guide that will ultimately benefit my daughters. *Girls, don't ever settle for someone who does not cherish you completely. You are incredible women and deserve to be treated with the utmost dignity and respect. I love you.*

Last, but certainly at the top of my list, I dedicate this book to my wife, Janet, the mother of my children. *You are the reason for all I am and all I strive to be. Thank you for giving me the best years of your life and making my life one to be envied by all. It's because of you that each sunrise brings new opportunity and each sunset new gratitude for another day well lived. I love you.*

TOC

INTRODUCTION

"Let the wife make the husband glad to come home,
and let him make her sorry to see him leave."

Martin Luther

I've invested much thought regarding what gift I could offer you, my sons, that would render the most significance and yield maximum long–term results both while I am alive and after my passing. Of all the presents I could bestow, this is the one I believe will be the most meaningful throughout your life. Consider it your blueprint for marriage. So many have joked about how you get thrown into marriage and no one gives you a handbook outlining what to do. Well…here you go. This book is a compilation of learning through experience. May it be a light to guide your path, an alarm to warn you of impending danger, a map to help you navigate your way, and a doctoral thesis to give you fuller understanding in matters formerly not known to you.

For some undeserving reason, God has chosen to bless our marriage with his divine favor. As of this writing, your mom and I have spent twenty–five blissful years together as husband and wife. Did I say perfect years? Hardly. Did I say we haven't had our share of tests and trials? You can bet we have. Did I suggest we were over the hump and free from future challenges? Not quite. Although you may have witnessed some trying moments growing up in our home over the years, I know you would unequivocally testify that those were the exception and not the rule. You could truthfully declare that your parents' marriage is one of the classic love stories—if not the best—that you have ever seen. And that says a lot, seeing that you have had front–row seats as well as backstage passes to the main event that has been playing all these years.

More than anything else I could ever grant you—including fame, power, or fortune—keys to a great marriage are what I offer you, for it is in that primary relationship where you can love and be loved, inspiring you to greatness and fulfillment. And believe me when I tell you that you can have it! Don't settle for anything less. I choose to pass this legacy along to you. Take the torch and run. I give to you the gift of knowing how to have a completely satisfying marriage.

"I am nothing special; just a common man with common thoughts, and I've led a common life.

There are no monuments dedicated to me and my name will soon be forgotten. But in one respect I have succeeded as gloriously as anyone who's ever lived: I've loved another with all my heart and soul; and to me, this has always been enough."

James Garner, from the movie *The Notebook*

It's not as mysterious as some want to make it out to be. And for sure, you will need to learn how to take an offensive pose to make certain that it happens, rather than a defensive posture hoping that happiness comes your way. You choose whether to be a thermometer or a thermostat in your marriage. A thermometer simply reads the temperature in the room and passively coexists, whereas a thermostat sets what that temperature should be. Thermostats are agents of change, able to modify their environment.

Many would say that life is short—here today, gone tomorrow. And I wholeheartedly agree. But when it comes to your marriage, life can often feel very long and full of crazy instants. Each day is comprised of countless isolated moments that can seem like eternity. Crises can evoke unpredictable reactions and emotions. We are all prone to mood swings and fickle changes in attitude. The everyday challenges of routine can require a disciplined stick-to-itiveness only found by reaching down deep within or putting yourself on cruise control to get through it.

Whatever the case, I have learned many principles, sometimes through the school of hard knocks, that I would like to attempt to pass along to you. Please accept this humble offering as my gift of love. I do not know it all, nor do I pretend to be an expert. But if there is anything good that I can pass along to you, I thank God for his grace gift to your mom and me. Our marriage is far from perfect, and I realize that we place ourselves in the proverbial fishbowl for all to see once we stand up and start talking about our marriage. But we are not talking about ourselves so that we can be noticed; instead, we are willing to become transparent so that you can gain a deeper understanding into why things have worked out fabulously for us. I'd rather you learn these things from me—whose life and love you've experienced firsthand—than from a stranger whose marriage you cannot measure.

I remember a friend telling me that he was having marital challenges, so he was going to see his minister for counseling. Just over two months later his pastor got divorced. What a travesty! Not that divorce occurred amongst the clergy, but that his minister was sitting in a seat of authority, offering experiential advice that was not working in his own life. My friend became even more disenchanted with his marriage than when he first started.

There are so many books out there advertising relationship advice. Where would you even begin to pick up the one offering the best counsel? How would you sift through those voluminous libraries of information to find the one most relevant for you? Moreover, how can you judge the content without seeing if it has worked for its author? In my humble opinion, the writer's own marriage becomes the litmus test for the book's authenticity and whether or not you can consider it a reliable manuscript. People don't want to hear a bunch of theories and pie-in-the-sky notions that haven't helped the writer in his or her own marriage experience. We want to know what worked and maybe even what didn't work. Tell us how you made it through or what caused you to fail. But at a minimum, tell us something that works!

No one can completely comprehend such a vast, complex topic as marriage. I do not have the laundry list of educational degrees and vocational initials after my name to automatically attract the interest and respect of the masses. But I have seen and tried things that work and don't work. I've done my share of research, topical reading, interviewing, counseling, encouraging friends, and, more than anything else, been a student of this matter so that your mom can have what she deserves in this life. Moreover, our track record speaks for itself. We are still completely in love! So, in essence, I feel qualified to at least convey my humble insights as a tool to aid in your learning.

While this book is targeted to my sons and sons-in-law—both present and future—it can apply to all men in general. If you are ready to step up and stop blaming your wife and take responsibility for making your marriage a union that others will want to mimic, read on. If you are prepared to stop the insanity of just coexisting and patronizing one another and to move on to excellence in your marriage, then this book is for you. If you are all set to reignite the embers of your first love and get reacquainted with the bride of your youth, then you are pages away from unlocking the keys to a successful relationship.

The information found on the following pages can add tremendous value to your marriage. Whether or not you choose to assimilate and implement what you read will be up to you. Like car keys left on the table, it will be your choice as to whether or not you pick those keys up, insert them into your car's ignition, and start the engine to begin your trip. So embark on your journey by committing to learn whatever you can in order to invest in your own marriage relationship. You are worth it. Your wife deserves it. And your children will be forever grateful.

Do you want a happy, fulfilling marriage? It starts with you!

A LOVE LETTER

"Love her your best now. You may not get a second chance."

Ron Biagini

Let me tell you about the most amazing woman in the world…my wife.

I was nineteen years old. We had a baseball game at the local park. Janet and I had just starting seeing each other. She was sitting with her parents in the bleachers, supporting our efforts. It was an intense game. As starting pitcher, I was involved in all the action. I went on to pitch a complete game, and my soggy, nasty, sweaty uniform was proof of the heated contest. When the game ended and I stepped off the field, Janet approached me to greet me with a congratulatory hug. Though elated to see her, I instinctively backed off, politely pointing out that she may not want to get that close to me and risk getting her own clothes wet and smelly. Without a second thought, she playfully mocked my act of selfless chivalry and quickly pulled me in tight for a bear hug. Having witnessed so many other couples handle this differently, I was stunned. I knew then and there that I had found someone special—the girl of my dreams—someone who cared more about me than what became of her clothes.

After what nearly became a three–year courtship, we married at an early age. She was twenty years old, and I was just out of college, not quite twenty–two. We moved farther out on Long Island and established our first apartment approximately forty minutes away from where we grew up and our parents still lived. Janet immediately became homemaker and domestic diva, keeping house and gladly attending to my every need and desire. I assumed the role of provider and protector, dashing out to work every day, counting down the hours to when we could be together again. To be completely honest, it felt more like a perpetual pajama party with my best friend than it did a grown–up marriage. After only a couple months of marital independence and thoroughly enjoying one another, we learned the surprising news that Janet was pregnant. Despite employing multiple forms of birth control simultaneously, it appeared that God had other plans and wanted to bring forth our firstborn sooner rather than later. With such a sudden shock, Janet could have been sorely disappointed in losing her freedom so young and early in the game, but she never once complained.

On the contrary, she was ecstatic knowing that there had to be a higher purpose for this gift of life that she carried and that she was about to be graced to take on the role of mother.

And so Rachelle entered our world, and we officially began our childbearing years. Within our first couple of years of marriage, I accepted a job transfer that took us from New York to Georgia. We were the first to defect from our families and move a thousand miles away from everyone. Again, Janet embraced the change and partnered with me to set up home for our growing family. Without the support of any local extended family, the responsibilities of motherhood rested squarely on her shoulders.

Our second child, Chad, was two months old as we took on this migration toward a new life down South. We intentionally elected to have our children close together in years so they could enjoy relationships with each other as well. After Rachelle and Chad were born, like clockwork, every two years we had another child: Chase and, finally, Chandler. Janet put on the many hats that only a mother can wear: nurse, homemaker, trainer, playmate, tutor, room mom, chauffeur, disciplinarian, and cook. To me, she continued as business partner, friend, lover, and so much more.

I watched her keep house, prepare meals, bathe and dress children, set up birthday parties, attend teacher conferences, bandage bruises, pull all–nighters with sick children at home and in hospital emergency rooms, cheer musical performances and athletic feats, host kids' guests, plan vacations, and take on odd jobs for extra money. On top of that, she continued to serve me as business consultant, confidant, companion, and everything else I needed. She was always willing to sacrifice her own comforts and extras for the good of the family.

After fourteen years of marriage, with our youngest child, Chandler, being six–and–a–half–years–old, we learned about a little four–and–a–half–year–old girl who needed a family. So Cheyenne was brought to us special delivery. Even though our platter was already full, I watched my wife love this girl—even with all of Cheyenne's familial and dispositional differences—as if she was birthed from Janet's own womb. And although that addition to our family was more challenging than we would have ever guessed it would be, Janet stepped up and handled it with humanitarian grace coupled with genuine motherly love.

Janet has truly stood by me for better or worse, through richer and poorer, in sickness and in health. We have lived lavishly, and we have rolled our coins to make ends meet. We have stood in welfare lines, and we have taken vacations to the Caribbean islands. We have lived in a sprawling home on the golf course in an exclusive gated country club community, and we have lived in a small inner–city apartment located in the ghetto. Like any family, we have endured highs and lows, suffered tragedy and trauma, only to have it draw us closer together.

I look at her today, and my heart still practically skips a beat as I see her smile lighting up the atmosphere from across the room. Her laugh brings life to me. Her poise captivates me. Her beauty beguiles me. Her warmth invites everyone to want to know her better. She is every woman's best friend as she immediately breaks down barriers and her transparency allows for her relationships to go deep quickly.

Her children are all so proud of her. She is fun and funny, up for anything. Don't give her a dare, because she will take you up on it. Not only has she kept her youthful beauty, but she works hard to maintain her girlish figure and dresses like a fashion queen. She is sexy, sassy, and so scrumptious.

I'll never know why my life has been graced with this one-of-a-kind treasure. What did a nineteen-year-old boy know about picking his future wife? For some reason that I can only call a grace gift, God let me win the lottery when he gave me my wife. Over the years people have asked why we got married so young. I readily respond that if God was handing you a fantastic, once-in-a-lifetime gift, would you readily accept it or tell him to come back at a more convenient time? I knew a good thing when I saw it and seized the opportunity.

If I had to do it all over again, without hesitation, I would choose Janet to be my wife and life partner. She has taken me further in life than I ever could have gone on my own. She has helped me raise the most incredible children who are destined to be world changers. I always thank and give credit to her for bringing honor to my name. Whenever people think there is something special about me, I am completely cognizant that there is another force supporting me and prodding me on to greatness. Her name is Janet, and she inspires me to be a greater person.

WHAT IS LOVE?

"Love is an irresistible desire to be irresistibly desired."

Robert Frost

Have you ever eavesdropped on the phone conversation of two young people newly in love? That's the great thing about being a dad. I get to recall many of my own adolescent memories as I watch and listen to my children take on their own experiences.

> *Girl:* "I love you."
> *Guy:* "Me too."
> *Girl:* "I said I love you."
> *Guy:* "I love you too."
> *[PAUSE]*
> *Girl:* "Do you love me?"
> *Guy:* "Yeah."
> *Girl:* "Why didn't you tell me before?"
> *Guy:* "I just did."

Girl: "Are you sure you still love me?"
Guy: "You know that I love you."
Girl: "But I love you more."
Guy: "No you don't."
Girl: "Then why didn't you say so?"
Guy: "I tell you all the time."
Girl: "But I always have to say it first."
Guy: "All right! I love you."
Girl: "Too late now. I already told you first."

Sound all too familiar? Ever wonder where all those phone–plan minutes are going? A two hour–long conversation of mumbo jumbo is really nothing more than just another excuse for those in love to spend time together.

What Is Love?

How do you describe a fleeting feeling? An elusive emotion? An idyllic age–old concept? For some it is euphoric, even utopian, a high like never experienced before. We hear talk of butterflies in the stomach, moonbeams in the eyes, wobbly knees, loss of appetite, hearts skipping a beat, yearning pangs, wanting to be together for hours on end, and timeless phone conversations usually expressing nothing more than mindless babble. The lovesick individual is completely lost when they are away from their lover. Just the sound of his voice or a peek at her picture is enough to awaken all the emotions. Ask ten people to define love, and you will get ten different descriptions. Yet we will all agree that it is something we all want, a castle in the sky where we all desire to travel.

"Love is that can't eat, can't sleep, reach for the stars, over the fence, World Series kinda stuff…"

Kirstie Alley, from the movie *It Takes Two*

When I first fell in love with my wife–to–be, there was nothing I would not do to express my love to her. There was no feat too daunting, no distance too far to travel, no request that I would not try to accomplish for her. During our courtship, I attended university and simultaneously held down part–time jobs to subsidize my way. One of these jobs was at a local twenty four–hour convenience store located not quite a couple of miles from Janet's home. Because of limited time availability due to my full school schedule, I had agreed to work the seven–at–night–to–three–in–the–morning weekend shift. When my shift ended and after cleaning up and clocking out, I would steal over to her family's house around three thirty in the morning. Turning off my headlamps well in advance, I quietly parked the car down the street and stealthily made my way past neighboring houses and into her backyard. A couple of taps on her rear bedroom window and she would wearily blink open those sleepy, yet beautiful green eyes. Everything in me came alive. Like prisoner and visitor communicating through bulletproof glass, pining for one another, we held our hands up to the window and imagined each other's touch while we lip–synched "I love you." Within moments of arriving, I was on my way home, energized to face another day.

I look back now and think, *What?! Was I a madman? I grew up in New York. What a risk! A neighbor could have called the police or tried to be a vigilante himself. What if her parents came to the window? What would I have said?* It goes to show that love is often crazy and doesn't always count the cost.

Dictionaries define love as: 1) a profoundly tender, passionate affection for another person; 2) a feeling of warm, personal attachment; 3) an intense desire and attraction toward someone; 4) a deep romantic inclination or sexual passion.[1]

But unless you've experienced that caring and romantic love for yourself, words on a page can never do justice to fully explain this mysterious virtue any better than authors, poets, and lyricists of time memoriam have attempted.

More practically, love is:

- Giving her the folded potato chips or the layered nachos that are stuck together.

- Letting her have the more comfortable chair in the Family Room as you watch TV.

- Allowing her to scrape and eat the burnt cheese left on the bottom of the pan.

- Opening her car door every time she gets in.

- Preparing her side of the bed just the way she likes it to sleep.

- Making the bed in the morning with all the pillows nicely arranged.

- Getting her coffee ready and knowing exactly how she takes it.

- Noticing and verbally acknowledging how nice she looks in her outfit.

- Running to the supermarket for groceries without playing the martyr.

- Putting the kids to bed so that she can have a much–needed break.

- Making all the arrangements for date night or an overnight jaunt.

- Doing all you can to reduce her responsibility load and stress level.

- Sitting still and enjoying healthy dialogue concerning the day's events.

The list goes on and on.

In "The Magic of Love," Helen Steiner Rice wrote: *Love is like magic and it always will be.*

For love still remains life's sweet mystery.
Love works in ways that are wondrous and strange
And there's nothing in life that love cannot change!
Love can transform the most commonplace
Into beauty and splendor and sweetness and grace.
Love is unselfish, understanding and kind,
For it sees with its heart and not with its mind!
Love is the answer that everyone seeks...
Love is the language that every heart speaks.
Love can't be bought it is priceless and free,
Love, like pure magic is life's sweet mystery![2]

Okay, we all want that. But what is it? Must love remain a mystery?

One of the most famous literary passages of all times recited at wedding ceremonies throughout the world is the biblical rendition of love found in the Apostle Paul's letter written to the Corinthian church.

> Love is patient, love is kind. It does not envy, it does not boast, it is not proud. It is not rude, it is not self–seeking, it is not easily angered, it keeps no record of wrongs. Love does not delight in evil but rejoices with the truth. It always protects, always trusts, always hopes, always perseveres.[3]
>
> 1 Corinthians 13:5–7 (NIV)

Many grooms listen to this all–too–familiar reading as they go through the surreal pageantry of their own wedding. His hands are sweaty; his knees knocking; his mind racing; a room full of witnesses stares at the back of his head and the soles of his shoes as he kneels at the altar. All he must do is robotically follow the minister's lead, echo some vows, and survive the ceremony. But in all the emotional congestion of the moment, does he actually understand what he is committing to? Does the groom really hear and comprehend what he has just pledged?

Patronize me for the moment as I take the above reading, personalize, and paraphrase it so that men everywhere, particularly husbands, can better understand and maybe even absorb what they are promising their new wife "until death do us part." A contemporary rendering might sound something like this:

> Love is patient.
> *I will hang in there as long as it takes—whatever the matter—and never give up on you. I won't pick on all those little things that might bother me or point out your imperfections.*
>
> Love is kind.
> *I will be kind and creatively thoughtful toward you at all times. Others will take notice of my gentleness and consideration toward you.*
>
> Love does not envy.
> *I will not exhibit any jealous tendencies that could make you feel uncomfortable, nor give you justifiable reason to be jealous toward me.*

Love does not boast.
I won't ever strut around like a proud peacock or sing my own praises.

Love is not proud.
I will not act conceited or behave arrogantly. I will be quick to humble myself and apologize without expecting you to reciprocate.

Love is not rude.
I will never knowingly embarrass you by acting obnoxiously or unmannerly. I won't make you the butt of my jokes to get a laugh from others—even if I am only kidding.

Love is not self–seeking.
I will consciously put your interests ahead of mine.

Love is not easily angered.
I will not be quick to get angry but will attempt to understand you better, knowing that I am far from perfect myself.

Love keeps no record of wrongs.
I promise never to keep a scorecard of your faults or bring up your past mistakes but to forgive and forget as best as I can.

Love does not delight in evil.
I will not derive satisfaction from your mess–ups but will try to help remedy the situation.

Love rejoices in the truth.
I will choose to celebrate whenever you do well or when you're right—even if it means that I'm wrong.

Love always protects.
I will go out of my way to make you feel secure and safe.

Love always trusts.
I will always believe in you.

Love always hopes.
I will strive to bring out the best in you so that you can reach your full potential.

Love always perseveres.
I will hang in there with you to the bitter end, being your greatest defender. Our love will prevail and survive the test of time. Others can look on and count on us to succeed. You have my word on this.

Okay...take a deep breath. Are you still ready to get married, knowing in advance what you are promising? Does this sound impossible? Actually, it's not, but are you willing to make that level of commitment to your marriage without any expectations in return?

What I find intriguing is the order of adjectives used by the author of this love letter as he penned his celebrated narrative. He starts out with, "Love is patient." Of all the other facets that love incorporates, why lead off with patience? Do you think that is intentional or just a coincidence? Ever notice when you quote something, it is always easiest to remember the front end of a lengthy passage? Then your memory fades and you start trailing off. Consider the following...

Gettysburg Address: "Four score and seven years ago our fathers brought forth on this continent a new nation..."[4]

U.S. Constitution–Preamble: "We the people of the United States, in order to form a more perfect union, establish..."[5]

Twelve Days of Christmas: "On the first day of Christmas my true love gave to me, a partridge in a pear tree..."[6] By the time you get to the seventh and eighth days of Christmas, unless you have previously performed this carol, like most of us, you have no idea what to sing about. And if you do, you can't remember what gift was given on which day!

In my mind the writer is trying to convey a beautiful message dealing with the embodiment of love. At the same time, he is mindful of prioritization, so that if the reader remembers nothing else, you will at least remember to be patient in your love. Ask any parent or teacher of a handicapped child if patience in love is necessary. Anne Sullivan, herself visually impaired and only twenty years old, was given charge of a deaf–blind student named Helen Keller. For the next nearly fifty years, Anne not only patiently taught Helen, but inspired and challenged her to greatness. Because of the patience of a loving teacher, Helen Keller became the first deaf–blind person to graduate from college and will be long remembered for her accomplishments as an author, activist, and lecturer.

"Marriage...requires a lot of patience."

Marriage, too, requires a lot of patience. That's the way our love usually starts out toward one another. And then, as though we have already bagged the game, caught the big fish, conquered the mountain, gotten the trophy, won the prize, we no longer treat the object of our affection with the same endearment we once exuded. Instead, we grow impatient with all those little things they do (or don't do)—things we once thought were adorable or perhaps didn't know about. Know in advance that your wife will not always do things the way you like them done or within your expected time parameters. Her habits may even drive you nuts. She may nag or misplace the keys. She may forget to give you your phone messages. She might actually enjoy picking your zits and telling you it's sexual foreplay. (Ask me how I know this...) She might take an hour longer to get ready to go out than you do. She may not agree with your thoughts on disciplining the kids. She might not have the same sexual drive as you. (All right, let's be honest: She *will not* have the same sexual drive as you.) She might not hang the toilet paper on the roller in the direction you prefer, or squeeze the toothpaste from the right end, or replace the bar of finished soap. Whatever those little nuisances are, patience will help you overcome. Besides, never lose sight of the fact that you are far from perfect as well and have equally annoying tendencies, though you might not be able to imagine any.

While there are many facets and stages to love, patience accepts your wife right where she is. It's laying down your own expectations and needs. It's helping your wife grow and get to the next stage. It's choosing to live at peace in spite of circumstances and challenges. A patient husband is an asset to the marriage relationship and exhibits great understanding. He can calm others down and brings peace to a crisis. He learns how to control his own temper. He exercises wisdom and avoids haste in his decisions. He can overlook petty offenses. He is able to persuade and influence others. He puts her needs above his own.

Seeing it that way, love certainly starts with patience.

MARRIAGE: WHY BOTHER?

"My most brilliant achievement was my ability to
be able to persuade my wife to marry me."

Winston Churchill

Those who are out there promoting the single lifestyle tell us there are certain key advantages to maintaining their singleness. Some of these include:

- You're not tied down to any one relationship.

- You don't have to obsess over finding that perfect match.

- You get to make your own decisions without interference.

- You have the liberty to play the field sexually.

- You have no one to answer to.

- You can spend your own money any way you choose.

- There is no one else to blame for mistakes.[7]

If being single is so alluring, then why do the majority still yearn for that special someone to marry? More than ever before, singles are creatively exploring more and more unorthodox methods to locate their special someone. Over a quarter of all Internet users in America have visited online dating Web sites. Revenue from annual online personal ads has tripled.[8] Moreover, an online dating magazine estimates that online dating is responsible for more than 120,000 marriages just last year.[9] I believe it's obvious that most of us want someone to love and be loved by.

Henny Youngman once said, "Do you know what it means to come home at night to a woman who'll give you a little love, a little affection, a little tenderness? It means you're in the wrong house, that's what it means."[10] All right, so maybe we shouldn't ask Henny. It saddens me to look around and see how many people are unhappy and unfulfilled in their marriages. Matrimony has become the joke of comedians, late–night talk show hosts, and syndicated columnists, and perhaps rightfully so. Society has adopted a "try–before–you–buy" mentality, as cohabitation has become an acceptable norm among today's youth. Couples now live together years at a time, some never marrying, due to the fear of commitment and failure. More than half the people who solemnly vow to stay together "until death do us part" end up breaking that very same pledge, some due to nothing more than a vague conception conveniently labeled "irreconcilable differences."

And statistics prove the divorce rate is even higher among those who have cohabited before tying the knot.[11] Among the loyal who remain married, how many are truly happy and fulfilled? It reminds me of the little boy who asked his father, "Daddy, how much does it cost to get married?" The father replied, "I don't know, son, I'm still paying."[12] It doesn't have to be this way!

Consider this humorous classified ad found in a local newspaper.[13]

> "FOR SALE: One 48-year-old husband. Never remembers anniversaries, birthdays, or special occasions. Seldom holds hands, hugs, kisses, or says I love you. Rarely is kind or tender. Will sell very cheap. Call 555–1655. All offers considered."
>
> Unknown

Although its mocking tone is obvious, the sentiment is practically depressing, as so many can relate to its message.

Marriage is a lifelong covenant. Certainly, there is a colorful assortment of factors and circumstances that can lead to divorce, but that is not our focus. I prefer to spotlight on how to have a successful marriage rather than how to avoid a failed one. Perhaps that sounds like a play on words. Is the glass half empty or half full? I choose to err on the side of optimism. I'm hoping to steer you far away from any predictable pitfalls and sidestep those avoidable traps so that you can navigate your marriage effectively.

What I want you to know, to truly believe, is that you *can* live happily ever after. Oh, don't get me wrong. None of us are faultless beings, so your marriage can never be perfect either. You can't take two flawed donors, unite them, and produce a perfect specimen. Relationship arithmetic has its own unique equation: half a man plus half a woman equals half a marriage. At best, your results will still be tainted. For many it may start out as a fairy tale, but reality will most assuredly set in, and you will have to deal with life and all its *mishigas* (Yiddish for craziness). But it can be done! And you can enjoy the ride. It's a matter of will and commitment, as well as acknowledgment of your covenant.

Ben and Molly were madly in love. They met while in college and decided not to wait to marry. The master plan was for Molly to put her schooling on hold and let Ben continue his postgraduate studies, the strategy being that if Molly could support their household now, giving Ben a chance to graduate, then he could finish law school, become a successful attorney, and provide for their family thereafter. In this way Molly's immediate sacrifices would pay long–term dividends. At face value their three–year plan made sense.

The first year went wonderfully, but then, like the sudden trip of a switch, something changed. Molly was growing increasingly frustrated with the lower–wage positions she had to keep and felt constrained to work multiple odd jobs to meet the financial obligations for their family. Ben never seemed to be home but was instead sequestered away with his fellow grad students, studying all the time. He was not available to sympathize with his wife's frustrations and pressure. She was not empathetic toward the demands of his education and approaching career. She felt tired and unappreciated. He felt no encouragement or support. What started out as a match made in heaven with expectations of eternal bliss was now in crisis mode within one short year.

Or take a look at Roger and Jean. Married for nine years, she finally conceived and gave birth to their long–awaited son. Up to that point, Roger had Jean's complete attention whenever he wanted it. They enjoyed traveling together as well as frequent dining out and experiencing new places. Both had been climbing the corporate ladders at their respective firms and reaping the benefits of a two–salary household income. But now they had a child. Jean quit her job, thus significantly reducing their spendable income. With parental responsibilities, lower earnings, and Jean always seeming tired, they no longer traveled, dined out, or had the sex life they once enjoyed when they were unencumbered. Roger felt neglected and resentful. He thought children were supposed to be an added boon to their home. Whatever became of their marriage?

> "Marriage is a union of two people,
> wholly committed to one another, to
> be life partners come what may."

Too many people enter marriage expecting their mate to meet their needs and to make them happy. If that is your belief, then you are destined for disillusionment, unhappiness, and a high likelihood of failure. Marriage is a union of two people, wholly committed to one another; to be life partners come what may. It is each partner being willing to give one hundred percent in spite of the other person's contribution. Through crisis and calamity, jubilation and triumph, you will carve out a unique history that only the two of you will share. However, these same two people by natural tendencies are inclined toward self–absorption and self–centeredness. Truth be known, people want what they want when they want it. Just take a look at an infant. Here you have the most innocent form of human life before they can even be sullied by the carnal influences of humanity. And what do they want? They want to be satiated any and every way possible. They want to be held, fed, changed, and given gobs of attention. And when they are denied, they will kick, scream, whine, and cry until they get what they want.

So right out of the start gate, marriage is already a colossal challenge dealing with each other's selfishness. Now combine that with some of the tremendous curveballs life can dole out, adding unexpected stresses and sorrows to any relationship: death, disease, illness, infertility, unemployment, bankruptcy, infidelity, handicapped spouse or child, to name a few. Without an uncompromising resolve, along with proper training and coping mechanisms, do couples even stand a chance?

Janet and I were so excited about setting up our own apartment when we first got married. We painted and decorated, bought some meager furnishings, and thought we were all grown up. And then, to our surprise, Janet became pregnant in our third month of marriage—despite using two forms of birth control! Because she had such intense morning sickness, we immediately lost her income, putting major stress on handling our monthly obligations. We decided to call in a favor with Janet's parents and asked if we could move back home and build an apartment in their basement. They graciously agreed, so we moved in with them and proceeded to live in Janet's former bedroom—right across the hall from her parents' bedroom—until the apartment was completed. What was supposed to be a two-week construction job turned into an eight-month nightmare as the contractor skipped away with our money and we were left stranded and confined to Janet's childhood bedroom. As quickly as it came, our newfound newlywed freedom was immediately stolen from us, as we were now captives in someone else's home.

Admittedly, things could have been a lot worse, and I am still very appreciative of her parents' support, love, and sacrifice, but it goes to show how life can deal some unexpected cards and you are left sorting out the hand. For those who have not been tested to the core of their beings with one of life's unanticipated tragedies, you might only imagine how this can exacerbate the already taxing demands on a marriage. Your relationship has got to be founded on an unwavering commitment to one another that, whatever comes your way, you will collaboratively work through it and come out together on the other side. You might acquire some battle wounds in the process, but you will still be proudly standing side by side, stronger than ever. The very deed of marriage in and of itself broadcasts to all that two intrinsically selfish individuals are now willing to lay down their own agendas and give themselves to someone else, the quintessential act of selflessness. So why is there so much failure?

Perhaps part of the problem is that so many people today get married for the wrong reasons. They marry because:

- They want the American dream of a family.

- Loneliness has a grip on them and they don't want to grow old alone.

- They want to escape an unhappy home life or undesirable living conditions.

- Family members are pressuring them. Maybe they've been dating for a long time or living together.

- Unplanned pregnancy occurs, and they now feel an obligation to one another.

- One or the other already has a child and now wants someone to help care for them.

- They need additional financial security.

- Immigration laws require it for them to stay in the country.[14]

"You are everything I never knew I always wanted."

Matthew Perry, from the movie *Fools Rush In*

I want to ensure that you enter marriage with your eyes wide open. While there will be numerous pleasures and privileges, there may also be many disenchantments and disappointments. I don't say that to set your belief barometer low, but to prepare you to realize that you will sometimes have to fight forward. One thing I do know: You can do it! This is especially true for those who were fortunate enough to see their parents happily married. In his highly acclaimed work, *Men Are From Mars, Women Are From Venus,* Dr. John Gray states it this way:

> A young boy who is fortunate enough to see his father succeed in fulfilling his mother enters relationships as an adult with a rare confidence that he can succeed in fulfilling his partner. He is not terrified of commitment because he knows he can deliver. He also knows that when he doesn't deliver he is still adequate and still deserves love

and appreciation for doing his best. He does not condemn himself because he knows he is not perfect and that he is always doing his best and his best is good enough. He is able to apologize for his mistakes because he expects forgiveness, love, and appreciation for doing his best.

He knows that everyone makes mistakes. He saw his father make mistakes and continue to love himself. He witnessed his mother loving and forgiving his father through all his mistakes. He felt her trust and encouragement, even though at times his father had disappointed her.[15]

But what about the young boy who comes from a broken home and/or did not have a fatherly role model? Can he still overcome the odds? Does he have a fighting chance? Truth be told, while the odds may not necessarily be in his favor, he can still overcome. For those guys, it is a matter of caring enough to learn what to do and what to avoid. Although you may not have had a positive male example in your life, consider the reverse spin. You may have learned from the opposite perspective of what *not* to do. If your dad was never around, or did not take the time to teach you how to treat a woman, or did not build you up, then at least you know what was lacking in your life and you can determine to fill those voids.

Success is a choice. And it is up to the individuals involved to do whatever it takes to win.

ROLE PLAY

"Marriage is not just spiritual communion; it is also remembering to take out the trash."

Dr. Joyce Brothers

Once upon a time, a beautiful princess happened upon a frog in a pond.

The frog said to the princess, "I was once a handsome prince until an evil witch put a spell on me. One kiss from you and I will turn back into a prince and then we can marry, move into the castle with my mom where you can prepare my meals, clean my clothes, bear my children and forever feel lucky for doing so."

That night the princess had frog's legs for dinner.[16]

We've all heard some variation of it. *We'll get married, live in a two-story colonial house with a white picket fence in the suburbs, have children, and live happily ever after.* Bringing unrealistic and even idealistic expectations into your relationship can kill a marriage before it ever quite gets off the ground. Think about it…If we didn't expect it to be nirvana, why would we bother getting married at all? And even though our parents may not have set the best example for marriage, we still concoct our personal storybook rendition of the perfect hereafter. In our minds we truly believe that she is going to be our missing link to happiness and that ours will be the love to defy all odds.

What is your role as husband? Are you the primary or sole breadwinner? Do you make the decisions? Do you keep the checkbook and handle the household finances? Are you responsible for the outdoor chores while your wife is expected to keep up the indoors? Is it your wife's responsibility to cook, clean, and bathe the children? I, of course, state it in this fashion because these are some of the traditional expectations within a marriage.

Now if you're asking if certain genders are more naturally inclined toward specific roles, then that answer is affirmative. Right from the start little boys make noises and want to punch, tackle, and kick. Little girls want to play dolls, and have tea parties, and talk on the phone. Men are known to be task driven and achievement oriented, while women tend to be more nurturing and relational.

Even with these innate gender differences, be careful of the expectations you force upon your wife so that you don't foster resentment. Whatever type of mother you may have had growing up, remind yourself that your wife is a uniquely different person. Just because your mother did things a certain way and was content to perform a particular role, don't automatically impose that upon your wife. Men often presumptively require certain stereotype behavior from their wives:

- She will have supper on the table at six o'clock sharp every evening.

- She will coordinate all domestic affairs: clean house, do the dishes and laundry, go grocery shopping, etc.

- She will be the primary caregiver to the children, handling everything from homework and getting them where they need to go to tucking them in bed at night.

- She will be dressed up and have makeup on and her hair done when I come home from work.

- She should be ready for sex anywhere, everywhere, anytime, all the time.

WHAT A WOMAN WANTS IN A MAN

Let's turn the tables for a moment. How would you like an insider's look at what a woman wants in a man? Do you think that could give you a competitive advantage like some athlete who's studied the game footage of his opponent? Would having a target give you something to shoot for? I've asked some women this question, and their responses include the following:

- He is head–over–heels in love with me.

- He knows how to meet my every need.

- He enjoys everything I enjoy.

- He is interested in learning my tastes and what makes me tick.

- He longs to be with me but knows when to give me space.

- He is good looking, has a great body, and is well groomed and well dressed.

- He knows how to conduct himself in all kinds of situations.

- He can take charge without bulldozing others.

- He is hard working, diligent, and capable.

- He puts me, our family, and home before anything else.

- He is a great lover, romantic, and sexually compatible—patient in lovemaking.

- He delights me with surprises on non–occasions.

- He is always telling me that I am loved.

- He builds me up and never tears me down.

- He can be affectionate without having sexual expectations.

- He communicates well and is willing to share his feelings.

- He is the spiritual leader of our household.

- He is quick to come to my defense.

- He makes me feel like I'm the most important thing in the world.

- He is completely honest and transparent.

- He is good to his mother without being a mama's boy.

- He is clean, picks up after himself, and puts the toilet seat down.

- He is respectful toward me and values my input.

- He is very involved with and loving toward the children.

- He doesn't define roles by gender but helps out wherever needed.

- He is generous while still a good manager of our finances.[17]

"Love won't obey our expectations, its mystery is pure and absolute."

Meryl Streep, from the movie
Bridges of Madison County

If that is a woman's wish list for what she seeks in a husband, no wonder our wives are left utterly disappointed after marrying us. Do you think you or anyone could ever live up to all those expectations? It's exhausting to even think about trying to fulfill that list. They are looking for Superman, James Bond, and Dr. Phil rolled into one. It's easy for us to excuse ourselves by complaining that their expectations are way too lofty and unrealistic. Yet as men we have many of our own preconceived ideas about how a wife should be.

MISGUIDED EXPECTATIONS

There's a host of unreasonable expectations that we bring into marriage based on our own preconceived desires as well as our experience of what we may have witnessed in other relationships. To expect your wife to live up to these—whether or not you ever communicate them to her—is an unfair pressure to place on her. Some of these marital myths include:

All we need is our love to live happily ever after.
Life brings with it many stressful scenarios. For newlyweds to believe that love alone is enough to handle any storm sounds quite romantic but turns out to be downright ignorant and sets their marriage up for failure. Couples need to develop skills to prepare themselves to stay committed in a lasting relationship that will have to overcome conflict, hardship, and challenges. Invest in the available pre–marital counseling and post–marital training to better ensure marital success.

She'll be different once we're married.

I've heard it sarcastically stated, "A woman marries a man expecting he will change, but he doesn't. A man marries a woman expecting that she won't change and she does."[18] The person you marry is the person you end up with. How's that for a no-brainer statement? If anything, the traits you see prior to hooking up are frequently intensified after marriage. If you expect to change her, think again. Either accept her where she is at or don't marry her at all. Rather than trying to change her, work on improving your own inadequacies so that you can better contribute to the relationship. When there's mutual commitment, what you'll typically find is that over the course of your marriage both of you end up evolving as individuals and transforming together as a couple for the betterment of your relationship.

My partner will complete me.

To suggest that your mate will complete you implies that you are an incomplete person to begin with. When two incomplete persons meet and marry, their relationship is still incomplete. The healthiest marriage begins with both individuals untiringly working on themselves throughout the course of their marriage so they may bring a sense of wholeness into the union. That way their lives together can complement one another rather than seek fulfillment from the other.

She will know exactly what I need.

Too often within marriage we expect our mate to be clairvoyant. We place unfair demands on them to read our minds, and then we get totally frustrated when she doesn't carry out our expectations. You have a responsibility to communicate your needs and desires clearly so that your spouse can fully understand what it is that you want from her. Anything less is setting her up for failure and yourself for disappointment.

Her job is to clean house; mine is to make the money.

Pigeonholing each other into stereotypes can often create frustration and squelch innovation. This is when it becomes essential to discuss your expectations of marital roles not only *before* tying the knot but also throughout your lifetime together. Develop a mutually agreed–upon game plan where each contributes their share to the greater good of the household, recognizing that roles can flip–flop at any time. Flexibility is the key.

Having children will strengthen our marriage.

How many times have you heard about a marriage on the rocks, so the couple decides to get pregnant, hoping that a baby will become the bonding agent that solidifies their relationship? On the contrary, children can actually drive a wedge into your marriage if your relationship is already unstable. When couples complain of working too hard and not getting to see enough of each other, the added responsibility of kids can sap any remaining energy you might have had for one another. Kids are great, but don't expect them to heal your hurts. Granted, you and your spouse may remain in the marriage for the children's sake, but issues swept under the rug will still be there unless dealt with.

We will have sex all the time.
In a society where the media freely broadcasts everyone having great sex at anytime, one would naturally assume that this should continue into the marriage bed. The reality is that work stress, kids, advancing age, diminished sex appeal, reduced libido, unpaid bills, and other forms of marital tension all factor into a couple's lovemaking frequency.

She will enjoy doing the same things I do.
Interestingly, a predominant need of men is to share recreational time and activities with their partner. However, if it does not happen naturally, it's not the end of the world. With some trial and error, you may have to search and sift out hobbies that interest the both of you.

Having money will solve all problems.
Someone once said, "I've been poor and unhappy, and I've been rich and unhappy. I'd much rather be rich and unhappy." The common denominator here is that the speaker is still unhappy regardless of the bank account

balance. While money may reduce certain types of stress, it will never be the cure–all for relationship woes.

I'm marrying her, not her family.
Guess again. Life has a funny way of bringing things full circle. Once Junior is born, watch how those in–laws you wanted nothing to do with come out of the woodwork like termites migrating to a new tree. While you might not expect to spend a lot of time with her family, holidays, birthdays, weddings, funerals, having babies, and other life–defining moments usually thrust even the most dysfunctional of families together.

DISCUSS YOUR EXPECTATIONS

Pre–marital instruction allows couples a platform upon which they can safely identify and discuss the expectations they bring into their marriage. It's okay to have expectations, as long as they are realistic and obtainable. If you are not fortunate enough to figure some of this out before marriage, then set aside ample time to talk about some of the questions outlined in the categories below. You will be surprised by some of the notable differences between you and your partner. If your responses are completely opposite, it's not the end of the world (or your marriage in this case). It simply means you have some work to do to understand each other's vantage point and to try to find an acceptable compromise.

Children

- Do you want any children? How many?

- How soon do you want kids after you're married?

- What would you do if you were unable to conceive?

- What are your thoughts on birth control? What type(s) will you use?

- What are your views regarding discipline?

- Who will be the primary disciplinarian?

- What type of schooling do you prefer for your children?

Parents / In-laws

- How often do you expect to see your parents once married?

- How often do you expect to see your in-laws once married?

- Will you still be expected to do certain things for your parents after you're married?

- If your aging parents become unable to care for themselves, where will they live?

- Will you entrust house keys to your in-laws?

Holidays

- What are your expectations for holidays and birthdays?

- Do you have any family obligations regarding special occasions or holidays?

- How much money do you expect to spend on gifts for each other for different occasions?

- About how much do you expect to be able to spend on gifts for other family members?

- What will you do if you can't afford gifts for extended family?

Illness

I propose that you can measure the health (or the degeneration) of one's marriage by the compassion or kindness we're willing to show each other as the years pass by. How do you treat your wife when she's not feeling well? Does the following hit close to home?

First year: The husband says, "Oh, sweetie pie, I'm really worried about those nasty sniffles you have! There's no telling what that could turn in to with all the flu germs that have been going around. I'm going to take you right down to the hospital and have you admitted for a couple days of rest. I know the food is lousy there, so I will bring you some takeout from China Palace. I've already arranged it with the head nurse."

Second year: "Listen, honey, I don't like the sound of that cough. I called my doctor friend and he's going to stop by here and take a look at you. Why don't you just go on to bed and get some rest? I'll tidy up the house a bit."

Third year: "Maybe you better go lie down, darling. You know that when you feel lousy you just need to rest. I'll bring you something to eat. Do we have any canned soup around here?"

Fourth year: "No sense wearing yourself out when you're under the weather, dear. When you finish those dishes and the kids' baths and get them to bed, you ought to go to bed yourself!"

Fifth year: "Why don't you take a couple aspirin? You might feel better."

Sixth year: "Whoa! Listen to you! You oughta go gargle or something instead of sitting around barking like a dog!"

Seventh year: "For Pete's sake, Carol, stop sneezing. Are you trying to give me pneumonia? You'd better pick up some tissues at the store. Oh, and while you're there, could you get me some ice cream?"[19]

- How frequently are you prone to sickness?

- How much sympathy and attention do you want when you are sick?

- How will you handle your spouse if they whine when they are sick?

- If your spouse was ever diagnosed with a life–changing illness or condition, such as paralysis or a debilitating injury, how would that change your feelings toward them?

Friends

- How much time do you expect to spend with your friends after you are married?

- Do you believe you should have to ask permission to go out with friends?

- How often would you like to entertain in your home?

- Does your partner have any friends you do not want to spend much time with?

- How will you relate to your opposite–gender friends?

- How do you expect your partner to deal with their opposite–gender friends?

Housing

- Where do you specifically desire to live (city, state, country)?

- What setting do you prefer (urban, suburb, rural, coastal, etc.)?

- Will you start out in an apartment, house, condo-minium, mobile home, or townhouse?

- Do you plan to rent or buy?

- Under what circumstances would you ever consider living with parents?

- How close by do you want to live to extended family?

Domestic

You may be the kind of partners who like to reverse roles when it comes to working around the house and yard. I heard about a husband and wife who chose to exchange chores around the house, including doing the dishes, which she hated to do, and mowing the lawn, which he detested. This worked to their mutual satisfaction until the self–conscious husband began to be bothered by people in passing cars staring at him as he relaxed while his wife mowed. He solved the problem by getting his wife a tee shirt to wear whenever she was cutting the grass. In big, bold letters it said, "It's all right…My husband does the dishes."[20]

- How clean do you expect your home to be?

- Who will be in charge of the domestic chores inside?

- Whose responsibility will it be for maintenance and upkeep outside the house?

- What kind and how many pets would you like to have?

- What will you do if only one of you wants a pet?

Time together

- How often will you expect to go out on dates with each other?

- What activities or hobbies do you expect to do alone? Together?

- Are there any activities or hobbies you expect to give up after you're married?

- How much time do you like to watch TV each week? What kind of programs?

- How will you spend your weekends?

- What are your expectations with vacation time?

Church / Religion

- What is your family's religious background and how devout were they?

- What is your religious affiliation?

- How often will you attend a house of worship? Which one?

- Will you continue to attend with or without your spouse?

- What are your thoughts concerning ministry involvement beyond attendance?

- How much money do you intend to give to the ministry?

- What if your spouse wants to go to a different church than you?

Grooming
- What is your favorite physical feature on your partner?
- How would you feel if your spouse gained a significant amount of weight after marriage?
- What do you expect your mate's appearance to be when hanging out at home?
- How would you feel if your mate wanted cosmetic surgery?
- What are your plans regarding physical exercise as a means to stay in shape?

Sexual
A husband asked his wife, "Why don't we try different positions tonight?" Without missing a beat, the wife replied, "That's a good idea...You stand by the kitchen sink and do the dishes and I'll lay on the sofa and fart."[21] Just because you're thinking about sex does not mean that she is.
- How many times each week do you expect to have sexual relations?
- Whose role will it be to initiate sex?
- How do you plan on achieving sexual fulfillment in your relationship?

- If you have different sexual drives, how will you reach a mutually satisfying arrangement?

- Will you allow for outside stimuli (movies, toys, magazines, fantasies, etc.) to enhance your sexual pleasure together?

- What if your spouse was unable to engage in sexual activity due to an impairment or physical injury or simply did not enjoy lovemaking? How would that change your relationship?

Financial

- What is your money or household income goal?

- Who will be responsible for paying the bills and keeping the checkbook?

- What will you do if your monthly income is not sufficient for your monthly bills?

- If you have to tighten your budget, what expenditures are you willing to give up?

- How will you come to decisions regarding major purchases?

Career

- Who will be the primary breadwinner?

- For how long will you both work outside the home?

- After children, what are your plans regarding working outside the home?

- What are your long–term career goals?
- Would you move if your mate were offered a great job that required relocation to a city you dislike?

DEVELOP A WINNING GAME PLAN

If you have a plan, you have a starting point with a goal in mind. Theodor Geisel, better known as Dr. Seuss, has written six books that are in the top twenty best–selling hardcover children's books of all time. The story goes that due to the illiteracy prevalent among school children, Seuss's publisher made up a list of four hundred words he felt were important to one's vocabulary and asked Dr. Seuss to cut the list to 250 words and write a book using only those words. Nine months later, Seuss, using 236 of the words given to him, completed *The Cat in the Hat*. Because of its simplified vocabulary, it could be read by beginning readers. Rumor has it that this same publisher bet Dr. Seuss fifty dollars that he couldn't write an entire book using only fifty words. Again Seuss succeeded, and this wager allegedly resulted in his literary children's classic, *Green Eggs and Ham*.[22] With a plan to conquer illiteracy and a goal to simplify enjoyable reading, Dr. Seuss was able to accomplish the unthinkable.

So what is it that a man wants in a wife? And how do you get it? Is it possible to even find? And how do you get her to do what you want her to do? Rather than itemize a man's wish list, think of it this way: A farmer plants corn in order to get corn. He sows wheat in order to reap more wheat. Whatever your wish list, whatever you want to see in your wife, begin by sowing those seeds yourself. Do you want her to speak respectfully toward you? Then speak respectfully toward her. Would you like for her to romance you and surprise you with her spontaneity? Then show her kind and thoughtful gestures that will produce that type of response. Do you want her to love you unconditionally? Then instead of pointing out her flaws and shortcomings, choose to build her up and accept her right where she is. Just as a farmer cannot expect a crop without the proper sowing and cultivation, a husband must give his wife the necessary nurturing to yield the optimal relationship.

Some guys just don't get it. Jerry would like for Eileen to discipline the children the way he thinks the children should be disciplined. Eileen is a soft-spoken, gentle nurturer who just wants everyone to be happy. Jerry is a strict tyrant who expects a tightly run ship, with everyone knowing their roles and performing their duties. If the kids do not perform adequately, then he wants Eileen to mete out the punishments. After all, according to Jerry, he's out in the workplace "bringing home the bacon," and Eileen is *only* a homemaker, so she mustn't have anything to do all day. First of all, Eileen does not even agree with Jerry's household rules. Secondly, his expectation that she will now carry out the consequences is completely against her nature. So what you have is a miserable wife, an angry, frustrated husband, and children who are confused. When a man asserts demands upon his wife, it can never result in a win–win.

> "Exceed her expectations of you while placing no expectations on her."

Exceed her expectations of you while placing no expectations on her. Work together to achieve the best household balance possible for the two of you. Take a look at how other successful couples operate, keeping in mind that although an arrangement may work for another couple, you may still have to tweak it or change it altogether so that it best fits your situation. Your goal in developing a winning game plan is to communicate, collaborate, and cooperate. There are no dictators here—just a husband and wife who love each other and are looking to zero in on a household routine that will benefit the family. Once you come to an understanding, remain willing to pitch in and do whatever needs to be done, even if it's not your "job."

BENEFITS OF MARRIAGE:
THE DELIGHTFUL DOZEN

"After all these years, I see that I was mistaken about Eve in the beginning; it is better to live outside the Garden with her than inside it without her."

Mark Twain

For engaged couples and those looking to get married, the following marriage benefits are a compilation of facts and ideals that you should absolutely look forward to. For those already married, I remind you of what you have within your grasp. Please resist the cynicism and sarcasm that can result from prior disillusionment. What you thought was going to be a "happily ever after" may have become an "I wish I never would have," but that does not negate the practical and potential benefits of marriage. It simply points out challenged areas where you may need to grow and learn. Marriage was never intended to be drudgery. It is not meant to be one's cross to bear through life or one's "thorn in the flesh." On the contrary, it should be a privilege and a blessing. And there are many benefits we take for granted that the married person enjoys over his unmarried counterpart. For starters, you have found that one special person who has agreed to share her entire future with you.

1. Marriage Is Exclusive

Two of our most precious friends, Don and Chrissy, invited us to their South Florida beach home in Boca Raton for a vacation getaway. The perch from their seventh–floor condominium balcony provided a breathtaking view of their private sandy beach overlooking the Atlantic Ocean. That week we were pampered like royalty as we toured South Beach and greater Miami in their convertible and were treated to lunch at legendary Joe's Stone Crab. We also took in the affluent Palm Beach and enjoyed a meal at a cozy Italian *trattoria* on Worth Avenue.

We were privileged to be their guests at the exclusive Boca Raton Resort & Club, offering a bastion of luxury, elegance, and indulgence. This resort offered hotel accommodations, gourmet dining, boutique shopping, golf, tennis, spa services, marina slips for boat owners, a half–mile stretch of beach access, along with cabanas and other beachfront and poolside amenities. Don and Chrissy's premier membership gave us VIP privileges during our stay. We had a chance to enjoy the resort's one–of–a–kind seafood buffet, swim in their distinctive pool, tan to our hearts' content, read a book while lying on lounge chairs, enjoy their private beach, and be waited on by all the servers who are trained to do nothing more than cater to the resort's upscale clientele. For us it was a trip that will be emblazoned in our memories.

"Marriage is an exclusive club…
Members only allowed."

Like that resort, marriage is also an exclusive club. As a matter of fact, this club is limited to just two persons—you and your wife. Members only allowed. Outsiders are not welcome or even permitted to enter. Furthermore, in this club you may not even invite guests; that's how exclusive it is! You and your wife are the only ones who can take advantage of its accommodations and amenities. You get to explore all the benefits and perks. You pay a one–time initiation by rehearsing your vows at the wedding altar. Your monthly dues are in the form of your continued commitment to this partnership. It is a high privilege to be accepted to this venerable institution. Not everyone gets invited, and only a committed contingent can endure the challenges of initiation as well as the trials of continued membership, but the rewards are well worth it. Your requirement for renewal is to make sure that your wife enjoys her club benefits completely and wants to continue her membership. As a matter of record, the highest praise is when your wife tells you that if she had to do it all over again, in spite of all the other clubs throughout the world, she would unquestionably join yours all over again.

2. Marriage Gives You Bragging Rights

I'll never forget when we first got engaged. Janet wore her ring proudly—almost intentionally always using her left hand to scratch that insatiable itch on her nose so that her engagement ring could be noticed. I was equally excited and actually wished I had a physical token of our engagement so that the outside world could visibly know that I was betrothed as well. For us, engagement meant that we were off–limits to everyone else and were solely promised to one another. It is certainly something to be excited over and to tell others about.

While I know we're to consider ourselves divinely blessed to find the right mate, having that right person by our side gives us instantaneous bragging rights. We have achieved a rite of passage that most people desire and even dream about. We now have the opportunity to broadcast to the world that we have found someone who is willing to share every aspect of her life with us.

Finding a good wife is likened to searching for hidden treasure. The closest I ever got to finding a treasure was when my dad sent me on a treasure hunt to locate a special Christmas gift. As we sat in the family room exchanging gifts, he gave me a written clue that led me to the bathroom, only to find another written clue. This one led to the kitchen, where there was a final written clue that directed me to the garage. Sitting there prominently displayed was the bicycle I had requested. That exercise was very exhilarating and built my anticipation for the final reward. When you're looking for a mate, you follow the clues of your heart and look high and low for the right person. There are obstacles on your path and counterfeits along the way, and it is your job to recognize the genuine article. Once you discover the right woman for you, it's as if you have struck hidden gold! Everyone who has ever fallen in love knows this feeling. I just wish we could all freeze–frame our euphoria and rehearse it when times get a bit challenging and struggles come our way.

Marriage is intended to be a God–sanctioned, highly fulfilling union. If it's anything less, take a look in the mirror and see what you can do to help set things right again.

3. Marriage Produces Companionship

A unique companionship is available to married couples who choose to appropriately exploit those advantages. There is no greater satisfaction than when a husband and wife can live harmoniously and deal with life as partners rather than adversaries. And there is nothing more fulfilling than having someone in your corner, even when the rest of the world appears to be against you. In a healthy marriage you have someone to:

- Sleep next to you so that you never have to sleep alone again.

- Act yourself with—through the good times as well as the bad times.

- Share your interests with.

- Love you unconditionally.

- Be your life partner, come what may.

- Take care of you when you need that little extra attention.

- Cheer you up.

- Offer input for decision making.

- Balance you so that you don't veer too far in one direction.

- Pray fervently for you when life gets a little rough.

Companionship within marriage can and should be wonderful. To always have a friend nearby is a huge benefit, and one we often take for granted. Your mate is available for quiet walks on the sand, tennis matches on the weekend, drives up the coastline, and window–shopping in midtown. She becomes for you an instant date for holiday functions, a card–playing partner, a confidant to share your heart with, and an advisor who knows you better than anyone else does. Whatever your interests, you have an automatic companion to share them with. Enjoy her!

Look at it this way: You and your wife are teammates. One is not above the other. No manager or coach here—just equal teammates. On top of that you have both signed a lifetime contract with this team—no kick–out clause. Neither one of you will ever accomplish a perfect batting average; it's impossible. You will witness each other's hitting streaks and batting slumps. You may have golden glove years where anything hit your way can be fielded. And you may have days where all you seem to do is make errors. This week you might earn your way to the highlight films, and next week you might make the blooper reel. In other words, just like you see in sports, your marriage will have wins and losses. But just because you have a bad day, week, or season, remember, there is always tomorrow; there is always next season. And with a little spring training and extra effort on your part, you can come back stronger than ever. After all, this is a lifetime covenant, and you might as well make the best of it!

4. Marriage Promotes Intimacy

Intimacy is so much more than lovemaking. It is having that soul mate by your side come hell or high water. It is sharing dreams with someone regarding your future. It is allowing another to know everything about you while learning all you can about the other. It is disclosing your most private secrets, knowing your mate can be fully trusted. It can be meaningful conversation or resting quietly in each other's arms without saying a word.

Statistical research reveals that married couples boast of greater sexual satisfaction over their unmarried counterparts.[23] In spite of ignorant comments and conjectures, having the same sexual partner for years can be fantastic. Relaxation and trust get to preside in your intimacy. If boredom visits your bedroom, that is only because you invited it in. Talk it out. Work it out. The marriage bed provides opportunities to learn and experiment together. You discover which buttons to press to stimulate one another. And you cultivate a predictable frequency to your lovemaking.

It reminds me of a story that I heard...A dad walked into a drugstore with his ten–year–old son. They happened to walk by the condom display, when the boy inquisitively asked, "What are these, Dad?"

His father matter–of–factly responded, "Those are called condoms, son. Men use them to have safe sex."

"Oh, yeah," replied the boy pensively. "I've heard of that in health class at school." He looked over the display and picked up a package of three and asked, "Why are there three in this package?"

His dad answered, "Those are for honeymooners. They will need those for their honeymoon night."

"Cool!" said the boy. He noticed a six–pack and asked, "Then who are these for?"

"Those are for newlyweds," the dad answered. "One for each day of the week and a day of rest."

"Wow!" exclaimed the boy. "Then who uses these?" he asked, picking up a twelve–pack.

With a sigh, the dad replied, "Those are for married men. One for January, one for February, one for March..."[24]

How's that for predictable frequency? Of course, the regularity of lovemaking will vary for each couple.

5. Marriage Enhances Personal Growth

There's a caveat to this: Marriage does enhance personal growth...if you'll allow it to. In order to achieve a highly satisfying marriage, there is a significant amount of personal growth that must take place in each partner. While some improvement may more naturally evolve as the relationship matures, much of it requires a concerted effort on the parts of the individuals. Marriage offers a platform upon which you are confronted with your own self–centeredness and forced to sacrifice some of your own wishes in order to help fulfill the needs and desires of another for the good of the relationship. For those willing to stay the course, you will be met head–on with opportunities to learn and implement all kinds of character–building skills. Trust me...

Spouses will be thrown into sink–or–swim scenarios and will have to learn how to negotiate and compromise, listen and communicate, resolve conflicts amicably, practice kindness, exercise patience, sacrifice, trust, forgive, or simply take one on the chin for the team.

You can be right or you can be happy. Rather than adopt an I–told–you–so attitude, learn how to get along and comply whenever necessary.

6. Marriage Increases Longevity

Unless you marry someone who plots your demise or plans your murder, individuals within marriage purportedly have better health and, ultimately, enhanced mortality rates.[25] Their lifestyles are more conducive to routine, stability, and accountability. A married person is given the charge to care for their mate that places an added responsibility on them that they must take seriously. I can't necessarily become irresponsible and carefree if I have other family members depending on my commitment and involvement at home. Moreover, they have another person who can take care of them. A little *TLC* can go a long way. Married men and women are also generally less prone to alcohol abuse and other risk–taking behavior, which leads to longer life.[26]

7. Marriage Requires Accountability

As much as we all may enjoy our independence and free spiritedness, marriage requires a unique accountability intrinsically necessary for the success of the union. The interesting paradox concerning accountability is the way you choose to view it. Within marriage there is a healthy form of accountability that is not only beneficial to the marriage, but also to the husband and wife individually. Some of the advantages of accountability include:

- Keeps you on the right path
- Shows someone you love them
- Promotes trust
- Demonstrates respect and honor
- Serves as a sign of maturity
- Keeps things out in the open

Although it's intended to be good, some may perceive accountability as a prison hindering them from their full freedom of expression and uninhibited enjoyment of life. If that's the case, don't get married! If you're already married, perhaps the accountability pendulum has swung too far in one direction.

Kevin and Rhonda were having marital problems. Kevin was very exasperated because he felt he was being unjustly suffocated by his wife's controlling grip. Anytime he was running late or out with a friend or on a business trip, she wanted him to call and check in to get an idea of his whereabouts and timing. If Kevin forgot or failed to do so, there would be hell to pay in the form of a tongue-lashing when he returned home. Truth be told, Kevin thought often about not coming home in order to escape the inevitable verbal abuse. At face value it appeared that Rhonda's dominance and control was killing this marriage and Kevin's frustration seemed justifiable.

What Kevin failed to promptly disclose was his unfaithfulness during their ten-year marriage. Not only was he a flirt, but he had been caught in an affair last year, and his wife was still reeling from that heart-wrenching discovery. As much as she wanted to trash the marriage when she found out, she was willing to give it another try, but it would be on her terms. And her terms required full disclosure and accountability as he slowly rebuilt her trust bank. Whose loyalty just went from feeling badly for Kevin to now completely siding with Rhonda?

There are several ways you can show accountability to your mate. One of the most obvious examples would be simple phone calls to let them know where you are and when you'll return. For us, whenever we had a serious discipline session with one of our children (which could be as simple as a "talking to"), we asked the other partner to be present. That way our anger could never go uncontrolled or the punishment would not be too extreme. It also let the child see their parents' solidarity on the issue so nothing could be distorted or manipulated. Accountability is a good facet within a relationship.

8. Marriage Builds Family Stability

Marriage allows for procreation. One of our God–given directives is to "be fruitful and multiply." Bearing children is a privilege and blessing from the Lord. Obviously, unmarried people can have babies too, but a marriage allows for a safe covenant for the planning of a family.

Being married is the best environment for building a stable family. There is a wealth of evidence to support that children living in two–parent families are significantly better off than those in single–parent homes. They are less likely to be abused or neglected, less prone to substance abuse and risk–taking behavior, and less inclined to drop out of school. These same children will exhibit higher school grades, loftier college aspirations, and overall increased emotional health. Furthermore, children from healthy two–parent families will typically continue the traditional pattern by seeking their own marital fulfillment.[27]

Raising a family as a husband and wife significantly increases the kids' chances for success. Parents know it's not easy to get up at night when children are sick, find the money to pay for shoes and braces and college, wait up at night while they return from outings with their friends, and then eventually let them go out on their own, leaving you in the sole companionship of the person you began with, your spouse. Ideally, children are better off having both a female and male influence; lacking one or the other may disrupt normal developmental patterns and social adjustment. While many single parents successfully raise healthy, productive children, generally it is easier and better to have two parents working together to achieve this goal.

9. Marriage Offers Financial Security

Why would you think research shows married couples as being more financially secure when we so commonly hear wives complaining about husbands squandering the money or husbands griping over their wives' spending sprees? As a matter of record, more than a third of marital disputes erupt over money.[28]

While marrying for financial reasons might seem shallow, the fact remains that there are several financial benefits available to married couples. For starters, quite often there are two wage earners who are more likely to pool monies together and invest in their combined future. The government offers all kinds of tax advantages and shelters to married couples. Married couples tend to be more likely to accumulate assets, purchase more expensive homes, save for retirement and education, and contribute to the economic bottom line.[29]

When one partner loses a job, the other is able to help sustain the family through tough times and financial challenges. Having someone to fall back on or bail you out can be a tremendous advantage.

10. Marriage Improves Household Support

There are so many responsibilities in life. Go to work. Put gas in the car. Pick up groceries. Drop kids off. Pay bills. Keep the house clean and the yard maintained. Attend meetings. Check on family members. Being married gives you a domestic partner for emotional and physical support. Whether it is cleaning house, running errands, or caring for offspring, two people who are willing to work collaboratively cut the workload in half. Unified, you are so much stronger than simply twice your individual contributions.

The problem is, too many of us defiantly cross our arms as we say, "That's not my job." We impose roles on each other without ever talking it out or recognizing the need for flexibility. "I'm not going to change Junior's diaper. That's her job." Or, "Why should I stop to put gas in the car? That's the man's responsibility."

Like a successful corporation, when all the players perform their functions collaboratively, then the business is able to thrive and be profitable. So it is with marriage. Adaptability for the sake of the partnership goes a long way.

11. Marriage Yields Shared Experiences

Shared experiences bond us to one another. Every day is another opportunity to create new memories. Whether it is a trip to Disneyland, caring for a feverish toddler through the night, or watching the sunset, sharing those unique experiences with your spouse is memorable and priceless.

Have you ever just sat together and reminisced about a positive memory or funny story? A few years back, our family got to enjoy a Caribbean cruise to the Bahamas. As part of our vacation, we chose an excursion that would allow us to swim with the stingrays. It sounded exciting enough. Let's try it! After all, the travel agencies wouldn't allow anything too unsafe that could risk endangerment and a lawsuit, would they?

We disembarked from the cruise ship and loaded onto a catamaran that would take us to our destination. After sailing for more than thirty minutes, we could hear shouts and shrieks in the distance that immediately roused our attention. Looking ahead, we observed people standing in the ocean, the waterline up to their necks, shuffling their feet while looking down into the crystal–clear bottom. Approaching, we saw scores of stingrays with wingspans of up to six feet and body lengths, including their tails, of more than ten feet! Our captain let down a ladder and told us this is where we were to enter the water and enjoy our interaction with these intimidating aquatic monsters and their venomous stingers. *Are you kidding me?* Because we had paid for this "death wish," I dove into the water, hoping to encourage the rest of the family to join me. All five children immediately sang in perfect chorus, "We are not going in!" My wife retorted, "Oh yes you are! We paid handsomely for this adventure. Now get in!" As they looked on in terror, one by one they jumped overboard and swam as quickly as they could directly to me, arms flailing and legs kicking desperately. The kids wrapped their arms and legs around my body, clinging to me for dear life. Janet looked on, laughing hysterically as she saw our children glued to me as I tried to maintain my balance in the water. I'm sure I looked like an octopus with all those human tentacles dangling from my body. When we finally looked about us and realized that others appeared to be enjoying this marine experience, each of us mustered the courage to stand our ground and cautiously address the stingrays. What began as a horrifying encounter quickly morphed into a very memorable and bonding experience that we still enjoy talking about.

12. Marriage Produces Spiritual Partnership

One of the most phenomenal benefits of marriage can be the spiritual unity shared when a husband and wife believe similarly. For one, you have a ready prayer partner who is available to you. You can be each other's spiritual covering. And you can offer a providential encouragement that transcends human understanding.

Rajesh is a Hindu trying to decide whether or not to marry a Christian girl. Rajesh and Sharon are very much in love. His parents expect Sharon to follow Hinduism after their marriage. Rajesh doesn't mind her following Christianity as long as he can participate in any of her church services whenever possible and she partakes in all the Hindu religious activities. Moreover, he wants to have a Hindu marriage and raise their children in Hinduism. Sharon is a devout Christian who is now torn between her spirituality and her love for Rajesh. Can you see how complicated things can get when two partners come from different faiths?

A common spiritual bond between husband and wife allows for a more cooperative sharing of wisdom, discernment, and counsel. Spiritual unity gives you an exponential advantage. As the two of you strive individually for an improved relationship with God, by default you will be drawn nearer to one another.

Are you ready to enjoy all those benefits of marriage for yourself?

FINDING MRS. RIGHT

"Happy marriages begin when we marry the ones
we love, and they blossom when we love the ones
we marry."

Tom Mullen

American author, salesperson, and motivational speaker
Zig Ziglar once said:

I have no way of knowing whether or not you
married the wrong person, but I do know that
many people have a lot of wrong ideas about marriage and what it takes to make that marriage
happy and successful. I'll be the first to admit that
it's possible that you did marry the wrong person. However, if you treat the wrong person like
the right person, you could well end up having
married the right person after all. On the other
hand, if you marry the right person, and treat that
person wrong, you certainly will have ended up
marrying the wrong person. I also know that it

is far more important to be the right kind of person than it is to marry the right person. In short, whether you married the right or wrong person is primarily up to you.[30]

I remember the day I first saw Janet. I was eighteen years old and sitting in my seat when she walked by. How could I not take notice? Every other head turned as well to catch a closer look as she confidently strode by in her tight-fitting designer jeans. She was the most beautiful girl I had ever set eyes on. Her facial features were flawless; her smile magnetic; her figure was perfect. And her long, flowing blonde hair commanded everyone's attention. Who was she? Where did she come from? Was she "attached"? I had to know...

Over the next several months, I sought out opportunities to ask around about her. I found out that her name was Janet, she was two school years behind me, and that she lived in a neighboring town. I saw her around a few more times and eventually got the chance to spend time with her in some group social settings, getting to know her on a casual basis. We talked a bit. We laughed a lot. We enjoyed our group camaraderie. But honestly, at that time in my life there was little motivating interest on my part (nor on hers, as I'd come to find out later) to move things forward. Regardless, she was dating someone else, so she would have remained off-limits to any of my premeditated advances. Although she did remain in my thoughts...

Time passed, and my interest in her started to grow—slowly at first, but with increasing intensity. Interestingly, at that young age and having just completed my freshman year at the university, I was really beginning to think seriously about finding a meaningful long–term relationship, so much so that I actually remember praying about it. My prayer went something like this, "Lord, I'm ready for a steady girlfriend. Not just anyone. But someone who I could really fall in love with and possibly spend the rest of my life with. Because you are God, I want your perfect will, but it would be really great if that person were Janet. Amen."

From that point on, my sights were laser focused. It was as though Cupid had shot an arrow through my heart, and I was determined to pursue my chances with this yellow–haired goddess. It would be nearly nine months from when we first met before we would hook up and go out on our first date.

"When you realize you want to spend the rest of your life with a person, you want the rest of your life to start as soon as possible."

Billy Crystal, from the movie
When Harry Met Sally

And let's talk about that first date...True to my diplomatic self, rather than step up and ask Janet out and possibly risk rejection (call me "chicken"), I nonchalantly told her in the presence of another female friend that we should all get together for a bike ride. Both girls seemed agreeable. I was ecstatic. However, I was already plotting my next move. Instead of planning an adventure for a threesome, I slyly decided to schedule that perfunctory bike ride with the other girl first so that I could then revisit the idea with Janet. So that's what I did. With that prior obligation out of the way, I could now approach Janet and let her know it was her turn. Pretty smooth, huh? (Feel free to refer to me as the "king of suave.") I phoned her, she readily accepted the invitation, and we commenced our bicycle ride to my sister's softball game, approximately three miles away. After showing our faces and going through some mechanical introductions, we were on our way. We continued on our bicycle ride to the local mall. Parking our bikes and locking them in the rack, we walked the mall and talked about everything under the sun. Our connection seemed magical.

Although we did not call it a "date" at that time, we both look back now and realize it was our first time out together alone. Moreover, it was in that innocent backdrop where we both began to experience the glowing embers of our first feelings of love for one another.

At my ripened age of nineteen years old, and she being just seventeen, we embarked on a love affair that is still impassioned to this day. We spent every moment we could together, and that was still not enough. This was the summer of 1981. I was entering my second year of college, and she would become a senior in high school.

Our subsequent dates consisted of bike rides, walks in the park, concerts, movies, church functions, social outings with our youth group, hanging out at each other's houses, and frequenting our favorite eating places and ice–cream joints. Whether we were holding hands on the bleachers while watching a baseball game at Tanner Park, sauntering the boardwalk at Jones Beach, or sitting on a park bench at some secluded setting dreaming about our future together, we thoroughly enjoyed one another's companionship. Truthfully, we could not get enough of each other.

Although I was relatively young, I had already learned some life lessons that accelerated my maturity. As the youngest of four siblings and privy to many adult conversations, I witnessed countless relationship issues—both good and bad—and had chosen to learn from them rather than repeat them. So it was very important to me to find out if our friendship was made of something solid and enduring before I dared to take our relationship to the next level. It was for that reason that I waited a full month before we even enjoyed our first kiss together. And realize this: we were spending probably some portion of six to seven days a week alone together, so that restraint was a Herculean challenge! Even at that early age, I intuitively knew that rushing into the affection part of our relationship could possibly blur and even dilute what our compatibilities were. It has been said that once you move beyond friends, should things not work out, it's practically impossible to go back to being just friends. Trust me…While I longed to be more than friends, I didn't want to blow my chances with the woman I believed to be the best catch on the planet.

Thankfully, our friendship had already been sealed and our temperaments meshed. We both knew we had long–term intentions for the relationship, even if we did not audibly communicate that to one another at the time. We lived in the moment and enjoyed our time spent together. As for our first kiss, I'll leave that up to your imagination. But, let's just say, it left me entranced and wanting more…

Will You Go Out With Me?

The dating years can be very stressful for you if you allow them to be. Just because it seems like everyone else has a girlfriend, never settle for someone just to be attached or to make you feel better about yourself. Find your own security and inner strength in who you are as a man, not who you're with. Josh McDowell has said,

> What you are as a single person, you will be as a married person, only to a greater degree. Any negative character trait will be intensified in a

marriage relationship, because you will feel free to let your guard down—that person has committed himself to you and you no longer have to worry about scaring him off.

So work things out while you're single, and make life easier for you and your future spouse.

"Find your own security and inner strength in who you *are*...not who you're *with*."

While being a couple looks appealing—and it most assuredly can be—remaining single has its own set of inimitable advantages, even if it's temporary.

While I don't want to sound like an advocate for singles, this can be a very special time in a young man's life. This is your chance to sow your oats and pursue your wildest dreams. Go to Hollywood and audition for that big role. Jam with your rock band buddies and see if you have what it takes to make the big show. Pursue your athletic aspirations, whether trying out for the Olympics or the local team. Travel through Europe. Climb Mount Everest. Camp out in the Grand Canyon. Snorkel in the Bahamas. Ski the Alps. Do missions work in Calcutta. Whatever it is that you have dreamed to do, now is your time. Do it! You may never have the freedom again to make such an independent decision. That's not to say that marriage is a ball–and–chain obligation preventing you from having fun by any means. There are simply responsibilities and accountabilities that must be adhered to once you are committed within a marriage.

Avoid making it your life quest just to find someone to be with. You'll be surprised how easily it happens when you are not obsessing over it. And if you're busily pursuing your passions, chances are you'll cross paths with someone who shares those same similarities.

In the 2006 remake of *The Last Holiday,* Queen Latifah plays Georgia Byrd, an employee working in the cookware department of a large department store. When Georgia accidentally bumps her head, she is diagnosed as having a rare neurological disorder and is given less than three weeks to live. Rather than lament her pathetic plight, she decides to make the most of her last weeks of life to do those things she has always dreamed of doing but been too busy or preoccupied to act upon. She quits her job, cashes in on her retirement savings, and embarks on a dream vacation to the Czech Republic that entails of a helicopter ride, extensive use of the resort's spa, snowboarding, base jumping, and enjoying meals prepared by a world–renowned chef. Georgia is totally revolutionized by her newfound freedom and transforms into a confident, ready–for–anything woman. It is in that condition where she finally connects with the man of her dreams, who has been in her life all along, yet she was previously unable to love.[31]

The moral of the story? Quit your job; blow your savings; take every risk imaginable and you'll find love around the corner. (Only kidding! That's Hollywood.) Carry on. Live life, pursue your dreams, hang out with your friends, frequent the right places, and treat others honorably. You'll be surprised how that special someone will just happen to appear when you least expect it. And you will know if she's the right one, because your internal monitors will bear witness.

Your mate will have strengths to complement your weaknesses. She will desire to please you. She will love your family, even with all their idiosyncrasies. And she will be secure enough in herself not to prevent you from spending time with them. She will make you laugh, as well as laugh at your jokes even when no one else does. (Ask me how I know this…) She will dream with you and agree to stand by you to help your dreams come true. And whether or not she is physically attractive to the rest of the world, she will be beautiful to you—inside and out. You will treasure everything about her, and she about you. Her eyes will twinkle. Her laugh will be adorable. The way she scrunches her nose will be the cutest thing you ever saw. Your interests will be important to her. Whatever she likes will be exactly what you will want to do. Compatibility will be a natural fit, like a hand in a glove. If she doesn't fit the mold, then run as fast as you can in the opposite direction.

Tyler and Nancy were as different as two people can be. He was from Long Island, a bit rough around the edges, accustomed to humor that included sarcasm and witticisms emitting from a strong Northern accent. Tyler enjoyed cars, sports, and being around people. He was a hard worker, didn't talk much about money, and kept his personal affairs confidential. He had a heart of gold and would give you the shirt off his back. Nancy was from a small town in the Deep South where everyone knew everything about everybody. Appearances meant everything to her. She wanted everything to be prim and proper and expected to be treated like the belle of the ball. She did not like socializing much, knew nothing about sports, and did not care for Tyler's family and friends. Yet this unlikely pair married. Can you guess the result? Disaster and divorce! Just because you make an emotional connection to someone at a party or are physically attracted to her does not mean she's a candidate for marriage.

Whatever you do, don't push yourself to date prematurely. I've seen too many parents who have not advised their children responsibly in this area. Truth be exposed, they are afraid to say no to their kids. And I've witnessed too many young people who simply weren't mature enough—emotionally and spiritually—who assertively ventured forth into the unknown of relationships, only to have their feelings trampled on and, frequently, their sexuality compromised. There is a balance to be found. That's not to say you can't have lots of enjoyment with someone of the opposite gender. If the opportunity presents itself, and she seems right, go for it! But guard your heart. It's one thing to invest your time, money, and energy in a relationship. But protect yourself from giving your undying affections to someone else's future wife. Preserve yourself. Practice abstinence and give your wife the gift of your virginity on your honeymoon night. Moreover, don't lead the girl on if you don't have intentions of moving the relationship ahead. While your charm, flirtation, and charisma may be cute, you are playing with someone's heart. Be fair and treat her with dignity.

On the other hand, don't be so rigid about courtship that you can't enjoy your dating years. If you want to hang out with a young woman just for the sake of friendship, then make sure the boundary lines are clearly marked and she fully assents with your intentions. But if there could possibly be more to the relationship, then go out and enjoy her. Sometimes the only way to make a fully informed decision is to take things to that level. I wish I could tell you that you will know she is to be your wife before you even start dating her, but it might not be that clear-cut. You may have to step out on a limb, move your relationship to the dating level, share experiences with private times and meaningful conversations before you can ever gauge if she is possibly the one for you. And if she's not, congratulations! That's a good thing. You figured it out before it was too late. Don't feel that you have wasted time and effort in this relationship. It's part of the hunt. You'll mature and grow in the process. Just make sure that you have always upheld her honor so that when the two of you move on from one another, you have not crushed her emotions or stolen her most intimate parts from her future husband. Contrarily, make it your intention to leave someone better off for having known you in the first place.

We have all had bad dates…but let me tell you about one that takes the cake. This shows you how tough it is to be single nowadays. This story aired on the "Tonight Show" with Jay Leno. Jay went into the audience to find the most embarrassing first date that a woman has ever had. When the eventual winner described her worst first–date experience, there was absolutely no question as to why her tale took the prize!

It was midwinter—snowing and quite cold—and the guy had taken her skiing in the mountains outside of Salt Lake City. It was intended to be a day trip with no overnight stay. They were strangers, after all, and truly had never met before. The outing was fun but relatively uneventful until they were headed home late that afternoon. They were driving back down the mountain when she gradually began to realize that she should not have had that extra latte.

They were about an hour away from anywhere with a restroom and in the middle of nowhere! Her companion suggested she try to hold it, which she did for a while. Unfortunately, because of the heavy snow and slow going, there came a point when she told him that he had better stop and let her pee beside the road, or it would be on the front seat of his car.

They stopped and she quickly crawled out beside the car, yanked her pants down, and started. In the deep snow she didn't have good footing, so she let her butt rest against the rear fender to steady herself.

Her companion stood on the side of the car watching for traffic and indeed was a real gentleman and refrained from peeking. All she could think about was the relief she felt, despite the rather embarrassing nature of the situation. Upon finishing, however, she soon became aware of another sensation.

As she bent to pull up her pants, the young lady discovered her buttocks were firmly glued against the car's fender. Thoughts of tongues frozen to pump handles immediately came to mind as she attempted to disengage her flesh from the icy metal. It was quickly apparent that she had a brand new problem due to the extreme cold. Horrified by her plight and yet aware of the humor of the moment, she answered her date's concerns about "what is taking so long" with a reply that, indeed, she was "freezing her butt off and in need of some assistance!" He came around the car as she tried to cover herself with her sweater and then, as she looked imploringly into his eyes, he burst out laughing. She, too, got the giggles, and when they finally managed to compose themselves, they assessed her dilemma.

Obviously, as hysterical as the situation was, they also were faced with a real problem. Both agreed it would take something hot to free her chilly cheeks from the grip of the icy metal!

Thinking about what had gotten her into the predicament in the first place, both quickly realized that there was only one way to get her free. So, as she looked the other way, her first–time date proceeded to unzip his pants and pee her butt off the fender.

As the audience screamed in laughter, she took the "Tonight Show" prize hands down, or perhaps that should be "pants down." And you thought your first date was embarrassing. Jay Leno commented, "This gives a whole new meaning to being pissed off."[32] Pun intended…

POPPING THE MAGIC QUESTION

"Don't marry the person you think you can live with; marry only the individual you think you can't live without."

Dr. James Dobson

After a period of courtship and dating, as you determine that you want to spend the rest of your life with this wonderful woman, getting engaged to her would be the most logical next step. This should be very exciting, as it is your proclamation to the world of your intentions to love and cherish this woman, to be wholly and solely devoted to her.

I trust that by now you have already met her parents and family and have spent considerable time in their presence so they have had the chance to size you up and assess your worthiness for their daughter. You've heard it said that when you marry, you marry the family as well. Whether or not you completely accept that notion, there is more truth in it than you may care to admit. Dr. Robin L. Smith, in her book, *Lies at the Altar: The Truth About Great Marriages,* discusses the concept of the Marriage Table. Rather than an intimate setting for two, the marriage table more closely resembles a banquet table of extended family, ghosts of dearly departed members whose influence will always abound, children from previous marriages, boss, colleagues, buddies, ex–wife, ex–boyfriend, clergy, best friend, doctors, therapists, and anyone else who may have held influence in your lives. Like it or not, these voices from your past and present, some louder than others, some remaining at the table forever, other cast members ever changing, become inseparably connected to your life as a couple.[33]

One of my favorite movies that encapsulates this concept is *My Big Fat Greek Wedding.* As part of her Greek heritage, Toula Portokalos is supposed to marry a Greek boy, make Greek babies, and feed everyone. Instead, she falls in love with Ian Miller, who is not Greek, and is a vegetarian to boot. Ian is an only child and is accustomed to a very quiet and private lifestyle. He is pleasantly introduced to Toula's large extended family and their over-involvement in every aspect of each other's lives. Ian's "Marriage Table" has just been dramatically expanded, and it now becomes an overwhelming fact of life that he is forced to contend with.[34]

Before popping the magic question to your future bride, be sure to get the blessing from one or both of her parents so they feel a part of this wondrous decision. Some may say that sounds old–fashioned, when in actuality it is respectful and admirable. It gives the family a sense of involvement and lets the parents know that you give credence to their opinion on the matter. After all, they have birthed, bathed, and raised this girl–turned–woman whom you are now intending to make your wife.

Be prepared for her father to ask some probing questions out of genuine interest and concern depending on your circumstances. Don't be defensive; be transparent and you will endear yourself to him. He just wants to know that his little girl will be loved and provided for.

That reminds me of a story:

A young woman brings home her fiancé to meet her parents. After dinner, her mother tells her father to find out about the young man. Obligingly, the father invites the fiancé to his study.

"So what are your plans?" the father asks the young man. "I am a Torah scholar," he replies.

"A Torah scholar. Hmm," the father says. "Admirable, but what will you do to provide a nice house for my daughter to live in, as she's accustomed to?"

"I will study," the young man replies, "and God will provide for us."

"And how will you buy her a beautiful engagement ring, such as she deserves?" asks the father.

"I will concentrate on my studies," the young man replies. "God will provide for us."

"And children?" asks the father. "How will you support children?"

"Don't worry, sir, God will provide," replies the fiancé.

The conversation proceeds like this, and each time the father questions, the young idealist insists that God will provide. Later, the mother asks, "How did it go, honey?"

The father answers, "He has no job and no plans, but the good news is he thinks I'm God."[35]

Make the engagement special. Every girl has dreamed about this moment her entire life, even to the point of acting out the parts with Ken and Barbie dolls. Women imagine the perfect Harlequin novel scene where they are swept away by a medieval knight in shining armor. They want the right to boast to all their friends how much they are loved by their man by his act of generosity and ingenuity pertaining to this occasion.

When I asked Janet to marry me, I wanted to make sure everything was perfect. I found out that her father would be at a business meeting on the Thursday night before the weekend I wanted to propose. I went there early and spontaneously beckoned him into a side room in order to convey to him my love for his daughter, along with my wish for her hand in marriage. I asked for his blessing, he gave it, and I was ready to go. Oh, one catch! I made sure that he promised not to tell his wife, or there would have been no chance for me to carry out this surprise. If Janet's mom knew about the upcoming proposal, she would have clumsily given it away by making a not–

so–subtle comment to Janet, like, "Is that what you are going to wear tonight?" or, "Don't you want to fix your hair nicer before you go out?" It's not that Janet didn't always look impeccable; it's just that secret female communication code to let the other know that something is afoot.

I picked up Janet that Friday for our usual date night. And I was totally prepared with the perfect evening timed and mapped out to a T. I had purchased an engagement ring that she had previously shown me as one of her preferences while we casually window–shopped months earlier. Little did she know that I went right back, put it on layaway, and started making payments on it. By the way, make sure you know what she likes when it comes to the engagement ring. After all, she will live with that ring and that memory the rest of her life. You are making a public declaration of how valuable you think she is. Save up for the occasion. Because to a woman, whether she openly admits it or not, size matters—that is ring size, of course. She will proudly or embarrassingly display her new trophy to the world. I'm certainly not suggesting the bigger, the better, because I realize that is cost prohibitive for many. But do put some time, effort, and investment into selecting the engagement ring.

Given our routine, I thought of an ingenious way to present it to her. One of our customs while dating was to have gum or mints available should we want to have any close encounters of conversation (or make–out sessions).

Since neither of us were smokers, I would always strategically leave the mints in the ashtray so that they could be easily accessible. This evening I decided to remove the engagement ring from its jewelry case and insert it into the mint package so it would be readily viewable when she opened the mints. I then carefully placed the ring–in–mint package back in the ashtray. I could see it now…She reaches for a mint, and surprise—she would feel the point of her marquis diamond in its setting and let out a squeal. I was so excited that I could hardly wait to watch it play out.

We had a special song that we always listened to in which a man expressed his unyielding oath to love his lady forever. I had it cued up on the cassette player, ready to sing it to her, making all her adolescent visions of romance come true. I had a few other tricks up my sleeve, but let me tell you how it went…

I picked up Janet at her house and said quick hellos and good–byes to her parents, not wanting to arouse any suspicions or wait around too long for her mother to ask questions. We jumped in the car and headed out for our special night together. I waited for her to reach into the ashtray for a mint, but to my surprise—nothing! So I tried to prompt her by saying, "Do you want a mint?" to which she responded, "What kind?" When I told her, "VelaMints," she said, "No thanks. I don't like that kind." *Great! Now what?* I thought. Being the clever guy I am, I spontaneously asked her if she would get one for me.

Later on, Janet told me she was thinking to herself, *What's the matter? Your arm broke and can't reach one for yourself? They're right in front of you.* (That's my spunky girl!) Thankfully, she had restraint and replied, "Sure, I'll get you one." Janet reached into the wrapper, discovered its hidden treasure, and started to cry tears of joy. I pulled the car over on a side street, popped in the cassette (yes, this was before CDs), and, through the lump in my throat, sang her our song while gazing into her tear–filled eyes. I officially asked her to marry me, she consented, and we both had a joyful cry together.

We then proceeded with the rest of our night. Rather than drive to what Janet thought to be our intended destination for the evening, I took her to a fancy Italian restaurant called Amato's in Amityville, New York, where I had made dinner reservations. It was one of those places we always talked about wanting to go to but never could afford on a student's part–time wage. She was elated. Inside the *maitre de* was expecting us, and our server was properly briefed regarding our special occasion. At my signal he brought out a balloon bouquet and a dozen roses I had preordered to the table. Janet was so excited and could hardly eat the meal or the specially prepared dessert that was about to cost me a couple of weeks of part–time pay. I comforted myself, knowing that I had made this the best night of her life—a memory she would not forget.

When we arrived back at her house later that night, we shared with Janet's parents the sequence of events that had unfolded that evening. Her mom feigned being offended that she did not know prior to the occasion and then sheepishly admitted that she would have most likely tipped off Janet in some way, even if it was just to tell her to dress a little nicer for our date. (Big surprise!) We all embraced and enjoyed the warmth of family.

Always remember to make memories that will last a lifetime. Here we are more than twenty–five years later, and I walked into our bedroom the other night and heard Janet telling the story of our engagement to someone on the phone. She told it giggling like a schoolgirl, revealing the pride in her heart as though it had just happened. That's when you know you've made a hallmark moment.

"Look, I guarantee there'll be tough times. I guarantee that at some point, one or both of us is gonna want to get out of this thing. But I also guarantee that if I don't ask you to be mine, I'll regret it for the rest of my life, because I know, in my heart, you're the only one for me."

Richard Gere, from the movie *Runaway Bride*

Ryan had big plans for his engagement to Katie. Because they both shared a passion for humanitarian work, he planned on making his proposal while on an excursion together to a third world country. When Katie's passport did not come through on time, his plans were foiled; all Ryan's hopes for the perfect proposal went up in flames. Now he was covertly holding a ring without the foggiest idea of what to do. But one thing he understood: he wanted the engagement memory to be special, so he did not rush forward. Instead, Ryan took his time and created a picture journal of selective special moments in their relationship journey together: photos of where they first met, first held hands, their first kiss, etc. On that special day, Ryan strategically sat Katie down. He gave her the photo journal as a gift, and the two of them read through it together, enjoying their stroll down memory lane. The final page in the journal was a photo of the place they were currently sitting, which happened to be the same bench where they had originally met. The caption read, "Where we got engaged." Perplexed and not immediately catching it, Katie looked at him, about to remind him that they weren't engaged, when she recognized the place in the photo was where they were at that very moment. With that, Ryan dropped to his knees and popped the magic question.

A little bit of creativity and preparation makes for a memorable experience. You can be sure Katie will proudly tell that story for the rest of their lives together. Do whatever you must to make it special.

BE A STUDENT

"If you would be loved, love and be lovable."
Benjamin Franklin

What kind of marriage do you want to have? Of course, no one sets out with failure as their primary objective. We all want a marriage that would be the envy of everyone— filled with passion, commitment, trust, companionship, sexual fulfillment, and you fill in the rest of the blanks. So how do you get there? Since there are no universities to attend that offer majors in marriage, how do you acquire the necessary techniques for what could easily be argued to be your greatest relationship challenge in life? Where do you find the tools to successfully venture into your marriage while preserving its meaningfulness and freshness along the way?

You must ask yourself if it is enough to leave the satisfaction quotient of your marriage to fate. Or is there something you can do to assume some control over your relationship? Is it enough to have a marriage like everyone else out there? Or are you hoping to distance yourself from mediocrity and stand out at your pursuits?

Take a look at sports…Many boys and girls throughout the world grow up playing basketball. What separates the average from the gifted? What distinguishes the one who excels from the rest? While some certainly have a more natural affinity for the sport, it still requires a greater desire, focus, and commitment to take the game from the playground to the professional arena. It's not enough to shoot a few free throws a couple times each week or to engage in casual weekend recreation. The one who has serious aspirations for success eats, sleeps, and breathes the sport, having the basketball practically attached to their body at all times.

Michael Jordan is widely considered one of the greatest basketball players of all time. Even for those who may not follow professional sports, his name is all too familiar since he has become one of the most effectively marketed athletes of his generation. Michael Jordan became known as a clutch performer who decided numerous games with successful last–minute plays. He holds an impressive résumé of accomplishments that includes leading the Chicago Bulls to three consecutive national championships that came to be known as a "three–peat." After a two–year sabbatical from basketball to try his talents on the professional baseball diamond, Michael returned to the Chicago Bulls. Amazingly enough, he led the team to three additional consecutive NBA championships, or, as insiders would say, he helped them "repeat a three–peat." Other honors include multiple–scoring titles, steals titles, All–Star Game appearances, Most Valuable Player (MVP) awards, and several other noteworthy accomplishments.

However, all did not start out so promising for Michael Jordan. As a matter of fact, he tried out for his high school varsity basketball team during his sophomore year and was rejected. But here's the key: if you want something badly enough, you will do what it takes to ensure those results. Rather than sulk and surrender, Michael Jordan continued to train and work out rigorously. Those efforts, combined with growing four inches over the ensuing summer, earned him a spot on the varsity roster his junior year.[36] The rest, as they say, is history.

"Our love is like the wind…I can't see it, but I sure can feel it."

Shane West, from the movie
A Walk To Remember

Or take music…Renowned classical composer Franz Joseph Haydn was born in Austria to working–class parents. Although his parents could not read music, they enjoyed singing together at home as well as with their neighbors. His dad was enthusiastic about folk music and had even taught himself to play the harp. Because his parents were perceptive enough to recognize their son's musical inclinations at an early age, as well as their own inability to provide him with any formal training, they sent Haydn off to live and apprentice with a relative who was both a schoolmaster and choirmaster. Haydn moved away from his parents before the age of six, never to live with them again. His intensive musical training and diligent studies as an apprentice would eventually pay off, but not without many personal sacrifices. He frequently went to bed hungry and was humiliated by the filthy clothing he was given to wear. He was even forced to work odd jobs, including that of a street serenader to make ends meet. Through years of persistence and perseverance and unyielding studies in his craft, Franz Joseph Haydn would eventually carve his own mark in the tree of musical history and become known as the "Father of the Symphony."[37] But consider the price he had to pay for excellence.

If we can be passionate concerning athletic and musical pursuits, how much more devoted should we be toward excelling in our relationships with our marriage being the prime focal point. Statistics tell us that one in two marriages will fail. Candidly put, that means either you or the person next to you will end up getting a divorce. And children of divorce have a higher risk of divorce when they marry and an even higher risk if the person they wind up marrying comes from a divorced home. So how do you make sure it's not you? Do you enter marriage flipping a coin and simply hoping that happiness will land on your doorstep? Furthermore, what makes newlyweds think they even have a chance at a great marriage when their chief instructor was their parents—and who knows how their marriage was?!

In order to be successful in any venture, you must become a student to learn all there is to know about your subject and then apply proven techniques. You must take time to learn about marriage and make your marriage of considerable importance to you. If possible, learn from an experienced marriage mentor or get the appropriate pre-marital instruction. It requires an intentional effort. But it also requires a fervent desire.

I played the piano growing up. Beginning in my third-grade year, my parents paid so that I could have weekly lessons—sometimes at the studio and other times at home. Those lessons required focus and fortitude. When I came home from school each day, my mom would turn on the kitchen oven timer for one hour. I was not permitted to go out and play with my friends until I completed that hour-long practice in addition to any homework assignments I might have had. I'm not saying that I liked it. Honestly, at the time I hated it! But learning requires sacrifice and commitment as well as desire. The problem was that I didn't *want* to learn the piano; my mom wanted it for me. And over time I gave up on those pursuits. Moral of the story: Equally important to performing the hard work is having the corresponding right attitude coupled with the want–to.

> "You've got to want a great marriage and be willing to do whatever it takes to achieve it."

For starters, you've got to want a great marriage and be willing to do whatever it takes to achieve it. Because truth be known, the condition of your marriage will be an exact byproduct of what you and your partner put into it. If people would just realize that you can only make withdrawals from your relationship account if you have previously made deposits.

J. Allan Petersen likens it to a marriage box and describes it this way:

> Most people get married believing a myth—that marriage is a beautiful box full of all the things they have longed for: companionship, sexual fulfillment, intimacy, friendship. The truth is that marriage, at the start, is an empty box. You must put something in before you can take anything out. There is no love in marriage; love is in people, and people put it into marriage. There is no romance in marriage; people have to infuse it into their marriages. A couple must learn the art and form the habit of giving, loving, serving, praising—keeping the box full. If you take out more than you put in, the box will empty.[38]

Heading into marriage, we each bring a personal responsibility to make intentional investments into our marriage relationship. An obvious approach would be to learn more about being a better husband or wife. So why don't more individuals take on this extracurricular learning mission to find out exactly how to do this? I've no earthly idea. But I do know that, as a counselor, the majority of couples that come to see me only do so after their marriage is on the brink of break–up. That would be analogous to getting your pilot training as the plane is out of fuel and nose–diving out of control toward disaster. This could have been prevented by taking some preemptive measures.

Landon and Hope hooked up and carried on a steamy love affair. When Hope became pregnant with Landon's child, they decided to marry. Landon had never been married before. His parents divorced while he was young and both remarried, so he was accustomed to the dad–stepmom, mom–stepdad dynamic. Hope also came from a broken home where her parents divorced when she was just two years old. Her mom was in and out of many relationships, had additional children, but never remarried. Her dad did remarry and started a new family. Although he remained in Hope's life, she never felt like she measured up and always felt like the outsider to her stepmom and half–siblings. On top of that, her dad was physically, verbally, and emotionally abusive to her. Hope had been married briefly once before and had previous children from different fathers who had all been given up for adoption. By the time Landon and Hope came together and agreed to wed, their only connecting link was the unborn child whose procreation they shared. With that background, what betting odds would you offer that their marriage be successful? Do you think their marriage stands a fighting chance without outside intervention? Not on your life! Yet this example typifies so many couples who decide to finally settle down and get married.

Additionally, think of all the potholes in your marital journey that you may have to veer around or intentionally take another road to avoid. We're told that the major reasons for divorce include:

- Money
- Infidelity
- Poor communication
- Change in priorities; workaholic
- Lack of commitment
- Sexual problems
- Addictions
- Failed expectations
- Abuse (physical, emotional, or sexual)
- In–laws or families
- Children or childlessness
- Incompatible belief system (spiritual)[39]

Do you have the necessary marital combat training to ward off attacks in each of these areas? How do you know where the enemy is lurking? And if ambushed, are you prepared to engage in battle without taking casualties or causing irreparable damages to your union?

For some serendipitous reason (which I now know to be divine guidance), early in my marriage I decided that I needed to know more about being happily married than what I had initially brought into my marriage. While I was fortunate to have parents who stayed married for forty years, they did not provide the example of a marriage that I wanted to imitate. My parents exhibited the stereotypical traditional gender roles of Father going off to work and Mother staying home to care for house and kids. Pop was passive and introverted. My mom wore the pants and was the household disciplinarian and decision maker. While I believed they loved each other, I never saw them display any open show of affection toward each other. And when they did, it was a quick peck on the cheek. Never did she sit on his lap or snuggle with him on the couch. He never caressed her face or nibbled on her neck. I never saw them giggle and whisper sweet nothings. Their sexual attraction for one another was top secret, and if I was ever questioned by an outsider, I would swear that their love-making was limited to procreating, which, in this case, would total five times (if you take into account her one miscarriage). Decision making was reduced to my mom making a request, Pop reflexively refusing, Mom begging, nagging, or crying, and then Pop finally agreeing.

Knowing that I wanted more than this for myself, I became an avid reader and learner about relationships. Since most real–life examples around me expertly exhibited what behaviors did *not* work within marriage, I wanted to know what *did* work. I couldn't get enough information. My circle of friends became my case studies. I even volunteered to teach marriage materials to small gatherings so that I would be forced to assimilate what I was learning and instructing others to implement. By doing this, I knew that I would absorb a lot of that information and that my wife would become the beneficiary of all my newfound principles and practices of how a man should treat his woman. The formative years for our marriage were founded on this pattern of learning and then putting it into action.

Become a student of marriage. Learn how to be a better mate. Get the appropriate premarital training. Find out about gender differences. Look around at successful marriages and glean from those relationships.

Where are the great marriages today? If you are married or plan to be, then choose to be successful. I'm not talking about wishful thinking; I'm talking about being willing to do whatever it takes to ensure your marriage's success. You can learn to be a great husband, lover, and life mate—if it's important to you. Be a student and have a great marriage.

Be great at what you do. While there are many talk show hosts, Oprah Winfrey has distinguished herself as a multiple Emmy Award–winning host of the highest–rated talk show in television history. Amongst all filmmakers, Steven Spielberg is notable for being the highest–grossing filmmaker of all time. Bill Gates, chairman and founder of Microsoft, is undeniably the best–known entrepreneur of the personal computer revolution. Greatness separates these individuals from their contemporaries. While cynics may argue that these had good luck or were in the right place at the right time, their commitment to learning their craft is what has elevated them to their apex of success.

How important is your marriage to you? And what price are you willing to pay to guarantee its success? Notice I said "guarantee its success" not "hope for its success." More pointedly, what kind of student are you willing to be to ensure the type of marriage that you want? Similar to the aforementioned examples, your desire, focus, and commitment will make all the difference in the world concerning your marriage. Those who desire excellence must take their learning that much more seriously and differentiate themselves from the pack. Having a great marriage is not just a dream; it is a real possibility. Actually, it's a responsibility—your responsibility! Take measures to make sure it happens in your life.

CAN SHE TRUST YOU ...

"Many marriages would be better if the husband and the wife clearly understood that they are on the same side."

Zig Ziglar

According to a *Reader's Digest* survey, the five most essential elements critical for a successful marriage include (1) trust; (2) time spent talking, laughing, and having fun together; (3) compatibility; (4) ability to resolve differences effectively; and (5) forgiveness.[40] Of these, trust ranks number one. More than communication or recreation, conflict resolution or forgiveness, spouses cite trust as the chief element crucial for a happy marriage. Without it, a thriving relationship cannot exist.

Then why are we such a distrustful people when it comes to our relationships? Because so many of us have either been directly slighted or have witnessed someone close to us get burned. Just take a look at the way society, media, and the movie industry added to the erosion of our trust levels. We now have our guards up. As the saying goes, "Fool me once, shame on you. Fool me twice, shame on me."

> "It was a million tiny little things that, when you added them all up, they meant we were suppose to be together...and I knew it. I knew it the very first time I touched her. It was like coming home...only to no home I'd ever known...I was just taking her hand to help her out of a car and I knew. It was like...magic."
>
> Tom Hanks, from the movie *Sleepless In Seattle*

Breaches to relational trust come packaged in many ways: lies, cheating, sneakiness, the blame game, infidelity, financial mismanagement, broken promises, alcohol or substance abuse, and various other forms of betrayal. Friedrich Nietzsche once said, "I'm not upset that you lied to me; I'm upset that from now on I can't believe you."[41] Isn't that the truth!

It is said that historical performance is a fairly accurate predictor of future behavior. While I've used that line in parenting my children to help them understand why I may not trust them concerning an impending situation, does it always have to remain that way? Although it may be impossible to rewrite history, is it possible for someone to earn trust back? Is there a way to draw a brand new line in the sand and start over again?

In this chapter we attempt to deal with just a handful of the areas where your trustworthiness can make or break your relationship with your wife. Rather than point the finger of responsibility at her, take the high road and consider your own accountability to the marriage. Can you be trusted?

...to always be honest?

When it comes to trust, lying is the kiss of death. Think about the last time someone lied to you. The next time that person says something—anything—you now have to process it through your dual filters of skepticism and suspicion concerning whether or not to believe them. That's a horrible way to continue in a relationship.

We have always encouraged our children to tell us the truth, the whole truth, and nothing but the truth. But kids will be kids, and even the best ones will occasionally test those boundaries. Leaving out a critical detail or embellishing the story to their advantage is not considered complete truthfulness. We likened it to making a batch of chocolate chip cookies using nothing but the finest natural ingredients. However, in the end, we decide to add in one spoonful of dog poop and mix it in really well before baking. Would you still eat the cookies? Of course, they respond with a resounding, "Gross! No!" So it is with telling the truth. You could have spoken ninety–nine percent truth and just one percent falsehood, but that lie (like dog poop) disqualifies everything else that was said before it.

...to keep your promises?

A trustworthy person does what they say they are going to do. If you make a promise, keep it. Your word is your bond, and it should be something your wife can always depend on. Maybe it would be better if you didn't say you were going to do something so you can't renege on your word. It could even be as simple as promising to fix the screen window over the weekend but never getting around to doing it. These little letdowns add up and diminish your credibility with your mate.

Arthur was notorious for this. Call it good intentions that simply never materialized. He frequently promised Sherry to do something and then just didn't follow through. It might be mowing the lawn, going to church, or running an errand. He claimed to be tired or that he forgot. Now whenever Arthur says he'll do something, Sherry rolls her eyes with the I'll–believe–it–when–I–see–it attitude. Our wives should be able to count on us and not have to guess if we'll be good to our word.

...to remain faithful to her?

A man should remain faithful to his wife physically as well as emotionally. Obviously, having an extramarital affair is not part of the original bargain when you first exchanged wedding vows. But there are more subtle ways that we can dishonor our marriage beds.

Craig and Vanessa have been married for less than five years. Recently, Vanessa has caught her husband surfing the Internet late at night, ogling various pornographic Web sites. When he finally does come to bed, Craig is primed for lovemaking, and Vanessa is totally repulsed by him. In her assessment, Craig is committing emotional adultery and violating their marriage covenant. Fantasizing about other women and then projecting those desires in his bedroom makes Vanessa feel like the object of his uncontrolled perversion. Because Craig is unable to connect with his wife sexually, he ends up frustrated or gratifying himself and losing the drive to be intimate with his wife, thus perpetuating their detachment.

If I had a nickel for every time I've heard some variation of the above scenario, I could retire on a secluded beach on Fiji. Your wife expects you to remain faithful to her. Why? Is it because she is an unrealistic, old–fashioned prude? Or is it because that was what you promised her in the first place—to be a one–woman man. You owe it to her. Monogamy does not have to mean monotony. Don't check out every other woman who walks past you on the street. Don't plot trading your wife in for a newer model. Be committed to the bride of your youth, and let her find security in your steadfast gaze as well as your unwavering devotion to her.

...to guard against outside relationships?

During our dating years, Janet and I shared a mutual friend. We all attended our church's youth group together. While Eric was initially my very close friend, because Janet went to school with him, she was able to independently forge a friendship with him as well. Soon after Janet and I first married, Eric knocked on our apartment door, looking to spontaneously pay us a visit. Because it was afternoon, I was still out at work. Janet opened the door and enthusiastically greeted Eric. Knowing that he was probably expecting an invitation to come in and visit, Janet preemptively addressed it by letting Eric know it would not be appropriate for her to let him in without me being present. He was aghast as well as insulted. She proceeded to tell him that not only would it look inappropriate to any onlooking neighbors, but also, out of respect for me, she would not invite another man into our home without me being there, regardless of the depth of that opposite-gender friendship. She could tell Eric was bothered by her decision, as though she were questioning his true intentions, which we all knew were purely platonic.

Although Janet and I had never discussed the possibility of that real-life scenario prior to it actually happening, how do you think her decision made me feel? You guessed it...Her effort to avoid any misconstrued appearances as well as her regard for my feelings carved a huge notch in the trust belt of our relationship that day.

Let her know that she has nothing to worry about by limiting your other outside relationships, particularly of the opposite–gender sort. Your devotion is to be primarily for your wife. And while you may not live alone on a deserted island and have no choice but to interact with others, your history, along with your present conduct, will be a clear indicator of your trustworthiness.

...to meet her needs for affection and conversation?

While trust may be the most critical element for a successful marriage, your wife has several other needs, including her desires for affection and meaningful conversation. Be there for her. As you will discover in later chapters, there is no one she would rather have fulfill these in her than you. Learn how to give affection with no hidden agenda. Decide to engage in conversation, knowing that it's important to her. Having her own needs met, a fulfilled wife is now able to take her mind off her own former relational deficiencies and, instead, focus her efforts on blessing the other members of her family. Your investment is a winning formula for all involved.

...to keep her secrets?

A young couple decided to wed. As the big day approached, they grew apprehensive. Each had a problem they had never before shared with anyone, not even each other.

The groom-to-be, overcoming his fear, decided to ask his father for advice.

"Dad," he said, "I am deeply concerned about the success of my marriage. I love my fiancée very much, but you see, I have very smelly feet, and I'm afraid that my future wife will be put off by them."

"No problem," said Dad. "All you have to do is wash your feet as often as possible, and always wear socks, even to bed."

This seemed to be a workable solution.

Meanwhile, the bride-to-be, overcoming her fear, decided to take her problem up with her mom.

"Mom," she said, "when I wake up in the morning, my breath is truly awful."

"Honey," her mother consoled, "everyone has bad breath in the morning."

"No, you don't understand. My morning breath is so bad, I'm afraid that my new husband will not want to sleep in the same room with me."

Her mother said simply, "Try this. In the morning…get straight out of bed, and head for the bathroom and brush your teeth. The key is not to say a word until you've brushed your teeth. Not a word," her mother affirmed. She thought it was certainly worth a try.

The loving couple was finally married in a beautiful ceremony.

Not forgetting the advice each had received, he perpetually wearing socks and she with her morning silence, they managed quite well, until about six months later.

Shortly before dawn, the husband awoke with a start to find that one of his socks had come off. Fearful of the consequences, he frantically searched the bed.

This, of course, woke his bride, who, without thinking, immediately asked, "What on earth are you doing?"

"Oh, no!" he gasped in shock as the stench of her breath overcame him. "You've swallowed my sock!"[42]

All right...so maybe smelly feet and halitosis are not the kind of clandestine skeletons in the closet that one can keep under wraps from everyone forever. Be that as it may, there is still no doubt that, as you grow closer to one another, you will uncover and learn many of each other's secrets over the years. Then suddenly a couple gets divorced, and all those little secrets become the tasty morsels of gossip that each reveals on the other to the entire listening world. Where is the integrity that we've pledged to one another? Don't anger or humiliate her by letting an outsider know about her most private details of her life. That is her business. And although when you married her it may have become your business as well, safeguard her dignity.

...to be committed to your family?

Commitment to the family can take on several faces. She needs to know that you will do the right thing, even when no one is looking or would find out, because that is what's in the best interest of your family. She also needs to know that your family commitment includes handling your share of responsibilities when it comes to running the household, nurturing the children, and even caring for aging parents. Be available to help out with whatever is necessary to keep things moving forward. A locomotive in motion requires much less energy to keep going than one that has to be started from the resting position.

Part of your commitment may include offering assistance around the house. We have an interesting morning routine in our home that includes making all beds before leaving the house. Of course, if we are going to expect compliance from our children, then we must first model that behavior ourselves. If I were to tell you that I frequently make the bed, you may not be very impressed—and you shouldn't be, because no one ever said that was the woman's job. However, if you're married to an interior decorator, making the bed is a beast of a completely different species. Our bed not only has multiple layers of comforters and custom-made bedding, in addition to the four pillows that we actively sleep with, we also have sixteen decorative pillows that must be strategically fluffed and placed in their predetermined rightful spot. The final touch is folding and placing the throw blanket diagonally across the corner on top of the bed for just the right finish.

"Date your wife and give her first place in your life."

I'm not sure if I can stretch the example of making the bed in the morning to being committed to your family, but catch the sentiment of the example. Be willing to do whatever it takes to prove collaboration and show teamwork. Coach your kid's ball team; attend their recitals; turn down invitations from outside sources if it would unfairly interfere with family obligations. Date your wife and give her first place in your life. As an actor may have but one performance to appease his audience, so you have only one lifetime to offer your family. Get it right and love them with abandonment so that there will not be room for any regrets.

...to provide financial support?

It is every husband's God–given mandate to ensure that his family is financially provided for. And while men are able to do this with varying degrees of accomplishment, as long as one is trying his best, that is all that matters. If your best can only provide for a mediocre lifestyle, then there is nothing to be remorseful about.

When it comes to our children's education, parents are always trying to encourage their kids to try their best and live up to their fullest potential. We can't expect a C student to perform A–quality work. So in that case, achieving C's can be completely satisfactory. But when an A–caliber student is obtaining B grades, then we know they are not performing up to par. Now we are not entirely pleased and must do what we can to coax that student to strive for better.

So it is with financial provision. It is not an indictment on a husband's abilities if the family is not able to live in the best of neighborhoods or indulge in high society's luxuries. However, it is a travesty if a man is not willing to strive for his highest potential and offer his best so that his family can enjoy life to its fullest.

...to take care of your own physical health and appearance?

After we relocated to Georgia and moved into our first house, we had to grow accustomed to subdivision–style living. This is where everyone belongs to the same community, and, intentional or not, neighbors begin to know your business. Since Janet was a stay-at–home mom, she developed budding friendships with other women in the neighborhood who were in similar lifestyle situations. One of these, Amy, used to stop over for a daily visit. After getting to know Janet and seeing how meticulously she took care of the house and herself, Amy asked why Janet dressed nicely and put on her makeup before I came home, rather than stay in her sweat outfit and tennis shoes. Janet politely let her know that I was in the corporate world around businesswomen all day long who were cleaned up and dressed up. Not that Janet felt insecure in any way, but she explained to Amy that if I was going to see other women who looked and smelled good all day long, then I should be able to come home and see my own bride looking at least as appealing. Of course, Janet looked and smelled a lot better than any woman I ever came in contact with at work during the day, but it is a tribute to the efforts we were willing to make for each other. Amy was enlightened and immediately put her newfound knowledge into practice, much to the excitement of her husband.

We have a responsibility to take care of ourselves, and our wives trust that we will do just that. Good physical health usually equates to longevity and a more active lifestyle with your family. Although some may deem it shallow, a pleasant appearance continues to promote the physical attraction between the spouses, further enhancing their bedroom confidence and sexuality.

Many men complain about the negative transformation of their wife's body after marriage. Perhaps when you met her she had the perfect figure—however you define that. You enjoyed those first years and remained recreationally active together. At some point you decided to start a family, or maybe it just happened. One child, then two, maybe more...Now that hard–bodied babe you walked down the ceremonial aisle with has the maternal markings of motherhood and, subsequently, may not have been able to shed all that baby weight. But when was the last time you looked in the mirror?

Rather than being so ready to point out her flaws, appreciate her for the price she has paid to build your family and carry on your name. Your encouragement may be just what she needs to get back on track physically. But whether she ever resumes her active healthy lifestyle, that's a decision she should feel free to make for herself without your harping and criticism. Love her right where she is.

At the same time, take responsibility for yourself. Part of giving her your best is to take care of your own physical health and appearance. My nagging question to men is, "Why do you work so hard to look your best and fittest before you are married, then, once married, you're willing to let yourself go?" The typical response is to want to blame her or to justify those lazy patterns we find ourselves so easily succumbing to. Although life may have its ups and downs, and stressful seasons may come that kindle unhealthy eating habits or interfere with exercise regimens, overall, and under normal circumstances, an individual must take control over his own body.

Too many men wait for divorce or the death of their mate before getting inspired to lose those unwanted pounds or to consider changing their traditional hairstyle and fashion. The indictment here is that we get too settled in with our wife rather than keeping things fun and fresh. Don't wait until you are "back on the market," needing to attract someone before you take action about your physical appearance. Shouldn't you be giving your wife your best now? While your quest to look your best should primarily be for you, do it for her as well. Give her something she is attracted to and can be proud of.

We admire ourselves through rose–colored glasses while looking at others through magnifying glasses. We should not have to second–guess each other's motives. "He was nice to me because he wants sex." "She had sex with me because she wanted something." We make excuses for our own behavior, but when we're talking about others, we leave no room for mercy.

Over the years I've told my children that trust is like a house of cards. Each time they carry something out according to plan, or they are obedient, or follow the rules, or make the right decision, that house of cards is built upon. But once something happens to break trust— even the smallest infraction—trust is destroyed, just like those cards crashing down into a pile of chaos. Now it must be rebuilt from scratch. Someone rightfully stated, "Trust is like a vase…Once it's broken, though you can fix it, the vase will never be same again." Broken trust results in suspicion, and suspicion cripples a relationship, usually resulting in its destruction. It takes a lifetime to build trust and just a moment to lose it altogether.

Never regard trust lightly. It should be the most highly sought–after treasure in your marriage chest.

PUT HER ON A PEDESTAL

"Love is when the other person's happiness is more important than your own."

H. Jackson Brown, Jr.

Janet is an interior decorator by trade. Because of that, I have seen my share of designer furniture, area rugs, window treatments, fabrics, and the like. We have shopped countless hours together for various home accessories, including pedestals of all shapes, sizes, and finishes. While pedestals can sometimes stand alone, they are primarily used to exhibit the item that sits on top of it. This may include collectibles, artwork, sculptures, or any freestanding item that deserves special attention or recognition. If you've ever walked through a museum or art gallery, you know what I'm talking about. Within a glass enclosure atop an ornate pedestal accented by soft lighting sits a priceless vase traced back to the Ming Dynasty. The pedestal provides a stage for that one–of–a–kind piece to alight upon. In essence it says, "Whatever I am displaying is very valuable and worthy of attention. Take notice."

Similarly, a husband should be aware of the important place his wife holds in his life and give her that due honor. Succinctly stated, he should place his wife on a pedestal. By doing so, he is portraying his wife as an essential part of his life and beckoning others to take notice. Whether or not the wife demonstrates behavior deserving of that seat of honor, it remains the husband's notable responsibility to make her feel loved and special. Just like the costly item on a pedestal, the wife on the arm of her husband ought to have that extraordinary recognition. The husband proudly claims her and exhibits her for all to see. He is communicating that she is valuable, priceless, and irreplaceable while treating her with the utmost dignity and respect. Can you imagine what effect it would have on your woman if you treated her this way?

Bill and Mary have been married for better than thirty years now, yet it is so refreshing to be around them. To hear Bill talk about his wife, you would think she had just discovered the cure for cancer or solved humanity's ongoing quest for world peace. He is quick to credit Mary for her qualities as well as her accomplishments as she listens in to his conversation and mildly blushes. It's just plain invigorating to see and hear his genuine admiration for her.

CHERISH YOUR WIFE...

The traditional wedding vows call for a husband and wife "to love and to cherish"[43] one another. To cherish her is to appreciate and show affection to her by placing a high value on your relationship so that you are willing to cultivate it however necessary. I cannot emphasize enough the importance of cherishing your wife. She needs to know that she is number one in your life. You might be a great provider for your wife, able to give her anything financially and materially, but until she knows you cherish her, everything else means nothing.

Dr. Gary Chapman, world–renowned author and speaker on relationships, wrote a book entitled *The Five Love Languages.* In it he reveals that every person has a primary love language, and often a secondary one as well, through which they receive love from another person. These include words of affirmation, quality time, receiving gifts, acts of service, and physical touch. It is your role to discover your mate's love languages and give love to her in a way that is most meaningful to her.[44] Here's where we fall short...It is way easier for us to give someone else love the way we want to receive it. In way of an example, my primary love language is "affirming words" followed by "physical touch." So the way I can most easily show love to Janet is to tell her I love her, pay her compliments, and hug her frequently—because that is what I need. While she may appreciate those gestures, they are not her principal love languages. She thrives on "receiving gifts" and "acts of service." Knowing that, if I really want to tell her I love her, I do it by writing out a card, leaving a note on the refrigerator, and buying a small gift to let her know I was thinking about her. Or I call her throughout the day, wash dishes, or put kids to bed as a way to fulfill her desire for acts of services.

To honor our wives, it is important that we learn to speak their love language rather than impose what we desire upon them. In doing so, we convey to them that they really are cherished.

BY THE WAY YOU SPEAK TO HER

As we'll explore in a later chapter, the quality and quantity of communication with your wife sends a clear message of what value you place on having her as part of your life. Not only is it important for relatives, children, friends, and strangers to observe how you honor her through your spoken words, but it is most important that *she* knows where she stands with you, even when there are no witnesses to your verbal exchange. The way you speak to her substantiates her importance to you.

She wants to know that you are willing to include her in your life and to share with her what's going on. Tell her about your workday, your colleagues, your thoughts, your plans, and your frustrations. Sometimes Janet and I will play the "Hi–Lo" game. We'll ask each other what the high and low points were for the day, and then we take time to talk about it. It's just another intentional way to initiate communication and maintain a strong emotional bond.

As part of your willingness to connect with your wife, learn to confide in her as your soul mate. Divulge secrets. Let your kids see you whispering sweet nothings in her ear as her shoulders tense up from a ticklish encounter. Bare your soul to her. It will be therapeutic for you and priceless for her. Share your feelings with her. Over a lifetime, men will come upon a host of experiences where it would do them good to talk it out with someone who loves them and knows them best.

Doug and Cindy went through a period where his consulting business was not making enough money to cover their household expenses. He was working long, hard hours but not seeing any results. He confessed that as a man this was frustrating as well as emasculating. Doug was confused, angry, and desperate, not knowing what else to do. On one hand, if he changed jobs, he would forfeit the years he had invested in building his company and lose any pending sales and renewal commissions. Yet if he remained in his role, he could not guarantee that business would turn around for them. Men are stereotypically the worst when it comes to sharing their emotions and prefer to keep things bottled up inside. However, Doug realized he needed an outlet and opened up to Cindy. She was not only understanding and supportive, but ended up tabling some excellent ideas that helped the two of them reach a satisfactory conclusion to their dilemma. It also gave Cindy some insight into Doug's feelings and insecurities, enabling her to be more sensitive and less micromanaging toward him.

Speak Kindly

Kind words are the overflow of a heart that is sensitive to another human being.

Praise your wife privately and publicly. It's wonderful to tell your wife how great she is, but it's absolutely phenomenal when you genuinely do so in front of others. It promotes her self-esteem and allows her self-worth to grow and flourish. I especially like to tell my in-laws what a great job they did raising their daughter—my wife—and how thankful I am for all their hard-earned efforts. As you can see, that kind word has multiple benefactors, as my in-laws and wife all feel the love. I also like to tell my kids what a great wife I have. It gives them security as they realize how much I love and value their mom. Additionally, it promotes solidarity in the home, sending the clear message to the children that they have no chance to divide and conquer us to promote their own agenda.

Compliment her frequently. Let her know how good she smells, how tasty dinner was, how much you appreciate her. I'm not telling you to lie and say something completely opposite of the truth. For example, if dinner was not that great on a particular evening, you don't have to say of the hamburgers, "I was wondering where I mis-placed little Johnny's hockey puck." Instead, you can say, "Sweetie, thanks for working so hard on dinner and making me feel important." You can always uncover a positive spin without resorting to sarcasm and hurtful words. Allow your words to reflect the honor you ascribe to your wife.

Speak Respectfully

All of us know how to speak respectfully to someone or how to demean them. Speaking respectfully includes being honest and open with your wife. Don't hide things or only give her half-truths; that is insulting and disrespectful and will never build relationship. Also, include her in the decision making—even if it's just small things. Build your wife's self-esteem and sense of security by asking for her input whenever you can. Watch your tone. Raising your voice at her or being sarcastic will only drive a wedge between the two of you. Rather, seek to draw her to yourself by the way you address her.

Part of communicating respectfully with your wife is listening to her speak without attempting to offer quick solutions. Some even theorize that having two ears and only one mouth was God's way of suggesting that listening is twice as important as speaking. Nonetheless, a woman's chief complaint is that her husband never listens to her. The reason this is so upsetting to a woman is because she needs to make her feelings known so that they can be deemed valid. It is incumbent upon men to listen well by giving her your undivided attention when having discussions. Don't try to solve her problem or give her advice. Listen with respect and empathy, thus telling her she's important and that you're trying to understand her as well as experience her world.

Respect and give credence to what she has to say— even if you have a different opinion on the matter. After all, she'll probably be right more than you'll care to admit. Her ideas and input are central to you having a successful marriage. By listening to your wife, you can learn things from a female perspective that you may never have thought of or been sensitive to. Janet has enhanced my understanding in so many areas. As she likes to remind me, she has put me in touch with my feminine side.

Speak Politely

Manners, etiquette, and politeness—these not only showcase your good breeding, but also impress the recipient. Growing up, my mom would always remind me if I failed to use proper etiquette for a situation. If I asked for something, I was expected to use what she referred to as the magic word, "please." If I received something, whether a compliment or a gift, saying "thank you" would be in order. I was required to say "excuse me" if I wanted to interrupt her conversation or needed her to move out of my path. Good manners are always *en vogue*. The point being that if you would exercise manners and politeness toward another female, such as your mother or a woman you pass in the grocery store, then be sure to say "please" and "thank you" and "excuse me" to the one you live with. Don't ever take her for granted or treat her with disdain. Not only do you have a responsibility for what you say, but you are also responsible for what you *don't* say.

Speak Gently

If you would speak softly toward another female, then start by gently addressing your own wife. If you would extend patience and understanding to another woman, then operate with forbearance toward your wife in what you say to her.

Have you ever seen a man overlook another woman's incompetence or error? Maybe she drops a tray of food in his lap at the restaurant or rear–ends his car at a traffic light. He gets out, surveys the damage, and, while annoyed, he good–naturedly laughs it off and acts like it's no big deal. But what if his wife was the one who dropped the dinner casserole or rear–ended another car? What would he say then? The real test of his marital genuineness is how he handles matters at home.

I remember when we lived in our first house. Rachelle and Chad were really young. Chase was not even born yet. Janet was going to back the minivan out of our two–

car garage. No big deal. She had done it a hundred times. But in her haste, she started the car and forgot to pull her driver–side door closed. (Don't ask…) So with the door halfway ajar, she reversed the car until she heard a loud crash accompanied by a tear. And all of a sudden, she realized what she had done. The open car door had ripped a hole through the dry wall of our house where the sheetrock enclosing the fireplace jutted out into the garage.

Amusingly, the reason for her rush was because she was getting ready to drive her friend Sue, who had been staying as our houseguest, back to the airport. You can imagine the ensuing chaos and mounting tension between the ladies. Wide–eyed and open–mouthed, Sue immediately inquired, "Will Ron be angry?" To be honest, I don't think Janet knew what to expect. Having never had this exact situation before, my reaction was yet to be seen.

Janet and Sue nervously bantered back and forth.

"You tell him."

"No, you tell him."

"No, he can't yell at you. You tell him."

The next thing I know, Sue is apprehensively walking through our house, asking me to step outside. When Sue told me what Janet had done, every notion rushed through my head. *How could you forget to close your car door? What's it going to cost to repair the garage wall and fireplace? Who do you think is going to handle getting this mess taken care of?* A zillion thoughts fly through one's mind in those following nanoseconds. Thankfully, what prevailed and came out of my mouth was common sense and gentle courtesy. I asked Sue, "Is Janet okay?"

I ran out to the garage and saw the driver–side door crumbled up like an accordion, the window glass shattered all over Janet's lap as she sat there nervously giggling. (Yeah…It's what she does when she gets nervous, and it does not help the matter whatsoever.)

So what did I do? I burst a blood vessel while screaming in her face, "How can you be such a moron?" Only kidding! I told her that it was no big deal and how it could have happened to anyone. (Okay, so I told a white lie.) I gently helped her out of the car and expressed that I was so thankful she did not get hurt. In disbelief, her tears turned to tears of relief, and she threw her arms around me. She has sung my praises for years with that story. Trust me…I haven't hit home runs every time at bat, but that one was a game winner! As for Sue, we called for a taxi to take her to the airport, and she ended up missing her flight after all.

Whatever you do, don't cause your wife to be afraid to tell you about a mistake she has made, because you will definitely make some boneheaded blunders yourself. You are her covering, her refuge, and the place where she should feel safest. I've seen so many women confide in their female friends about the things they feel they must hide from their man so that he doesn't blow his top. For sure that's a disgrace, but it is even more shameful if he would handle it more composedly if it came from someone other than his wife. As parents we teach our children how to restrain themselves in certain societal situations. Yet some husbands think they have the right to vent their uncontrolled temper at their own wife as if she is his inanimate property. Some husbands even want to control the small things like what she gets to watch on television or how much she spends on a can of beans.

Anytime Rosanne purchases new clothes, she conceals them in her closet for a while. That way when she finally wears it and Ted asks when she got an outfit that he doesn't recall seeing before, she can honestly respond with technical precision that she's had it for a while. Now if Rosanne was spending money that the household could not afford, then this example would take on a different tone. However, in this case, Ted is simply a controlling tyrant who doesn't like decisions—whether big or small—being made without his approval. For that reason, it becomes easier for Rosanne to behave in this deceptive fashion rather than receive Ted's condescending reprimands. That's not the proper foundation to build a relationship upon.

As men we need to practice a gentle civility when it comes to speaking with our wives.

BY THE WAY YOU ACT TOWARD HER

It has sarcastically been said that when a man opens the car door for his wife, you can be sure of one of two things: either the car is new or the wife is new. Break the mold and open the door for your wife for the rest of your life together. Why treat her with fewer honors now that she's been married to you for some time? Logically, it would make sense that she deserves even more respect now that she has put up with you for more years. Whether you are alone with her in a covered garage or on public display in a busy parking lot, open her door and send the message that she is worthy of special treatment.

It is a mockery to witness a man acting kindly toward another woman knowing that he's condescending and dominating at home. Why is it easier for a man to open the door for someone other than his wife? Or pull out a chair for a female business partner but let his wife find her own seat? Children get to observe this hypocritical behavior and recognize Dad sending those mixed signals. This should never be!

Don't ever treat another woman better than you would your own wife. That other woman has not washed your socks, sorted your dirty laundry, cleaned your vomit, borne your children, and cooked your meals. She has not gone through thick and thin with you, enduring your low points and mood swings. She has not been intimate with you and given you the most sacred parts of herself. What gives you the right to swoon, flirt, and coddle another when your most prized possession is already wearing your last name as her own?

"Don't ever treat another woman better than you would your own wife."

Character is who you are inside your own home. Don't portray yourself as one type of person publicly and behave altogether differently in private.

Lee and Alice had been married over ten years. To see them together would make you think they had a real, solid relationship. They attended all the school functions with their kids, sitting together like the happy family. Lee was friendly and personable, a very likeable guy although a bit standoffish. What you could not casually detect was the fear that Lee inflicted upon his family to uphold their blissful masquerade. In their home, Lee was a bully with an out–of–control temper. He frequently beat his wife and daughter mercilessly. They were forced to hide the bruises with appropriate clothing or sometimes even sunglasses. What initially appeared as a family that always wanted to be together was nothing more than a controlling despot not willing to allow his wife and kids out of his sights so they would not have opportunity to expose their regrettable plight.

Needless to say, men like this are sickening, spineless cowards who don't deserve the high privilege of marriage.

Treat Her Royally

Why is it that some men treat their woman like a queen before they are wed but then treat her like their property once they are married? What mysterious metamorphosis takes place pre– and post–honeymoon? Prior to being married, the man can hardly do enough for his bride-to-be. He buys her flowers, writes out his truest feelings in greeting cards for no particular occasion, skips football games to go shopping with her, and sits on park benches and porch swings just to hear about her day. It's as if he has been immersed in an estrogen bath. Then he places a wedding ring on her finger and some diabolical transformation occurs. Now gifts and flowers are limited to occasions—if he remembers. Football season becomes sacred. Backrubs are preciously saved and only offered to her as a manipulative precursor to sex. And conversations are reduced to talking solely about essential household matters: "How much did that cost?" "Did you iron my white shirt?" Don't ever allow your love to cool off so that it diminishes the level of respect you grant her.

_____

"Why is it that men treat their woman like a queen before they are wed but then treat her like their property once they are married?"

Other women should envy the way you treat your wife. Be a role model to your peer group of husbands. When all of your wife's friends tell her they wish their husbands were more like you, let it be a loud endorsement that you are doing the right things. But whether or not anyone ever witnesses how you behave toward your wife, treat her like royalty, knowing that she deserves nothing less. You hold the magic wand to make her feel like Cinderella and to allow her marriage experience to be wonderful.

A wife went to the police station with her next–door neighbor to report that her husband was missing. The policeman asked for a description. She said, "He's thirty–five years old, six foot one, has dark eyes, dark wavy hair, an athletic build, weighs 185 pounds, is soft–spoken, and is good to the children." The next–door neighbor protested, "Your husband is five foot eight, chubby, bald, has a big mouth, and is mean to your children." The wife replied, "Yes, but who wants *him* back?"[45]

When you choose to treat her like royalty, your relationship will go to a new level. She will love you and serve you because of your unconditional love toward her. She *will* want you back.

Put Her First

Give her first place in your life. Make sure she unequivocally knows that no one else even holds a matchstick to her. This includes your boss, your minister, your friends, and especially your parents. Prefer her even before yourself. Ensure that she feels special.

Early in our marriage I had a little conflict between my mom and my wife. My mom was putting some pressure on me to do something that was contrary to what my wife desired. I found myself between a rock and a hard place. Boldly, yet gently, I took the initiative to tell my mom over the phone while Janet was listening, "Mom, you know I love you, but I'm married now, and I love my wife and she comes first. Sorry." Janet unequivocally knew from that point forward who was first in my life.

As a general rule of life, learn how to put others above yourself, but especially practice this within your marriage. Some would say that you have to carve out your own path in life. If you don't do for yourself, no one will do it for you. While I understand the psychology behind that, in marriage you will quickly learn that the more you do for your wife, the more she is fulfilled, and the more your wife will end up doing for you. A quick postscript is in order here: Don't do for your wife just so she will do for you. That's called manipulation, and you will be tapping your feet, waiting for it to happen. Do for her because you are trying to love her your best.

Give her preferential treatment. Treat her like a VIP (Very Important Person). When the president is ceremoniously announced by the house sergeant at arms, the president enters the House Chamber to a standing ovation and spends the next several minutes greeting members of Congress while working his way toward the podium. The ovation continues incessantly during this time as the president hands out copies of the address and prepares himself. When the chamber finally settles down from the president's arrival and the attendees take their seats, the speaker then taps the gavel and officially presents the president to the joint session of Congress. Another standing ovation erupts before the president finally begins his address.[46] This preferential treatment is simply an acknowledgment of who the president is—not whether or not you agree with him.

Or maybe you have watched one of the Hollywood red carpet events—the Oscars or Golden Globe Awards. Actors are chauffeured in by limousines. They exit their vehicles to the flashes and lights of the countless paparazzi and other photographers. This is their moment to shine. Each star is dressed in the finest designer clothing and accessories as they are escorted to the event. Interviewers crowd in to ask them everything imaginable, from which designer's apparel they are donning to who is their mysterious escort for the event. Whether it's their arrival, the actual awards show, or the after–event parties, the treatment and attention lavished upon them is second to none.

While I may not give Janet a standing ovation when she enters the room, it is my intention to make her feel just as special. It is my quest in life to make her as happy as she can be. Now as quickly as I say that, I retract and clarify that I know I am not ultimately responsible for her happiness. Each of us has to find that joy within ourselves. But as much as it is in my power, I can add to it rather than subtract from it.

There's an old adage that says "If Mama ain't happy, ain't nobody happy. If Daddy ain't happy, who cares?" (I think my wife made up the second line, but I can't prove it.) Og Mandino said it this way: "Happiness is a perfume you cannot pour on others without getting a few drops on yourself."[47] By contributing to your wife's happiness, you will get to enjoy the overflow of a more peaceable home and fulfilling marriage.

Don't Compare

It's become a lingering joke between my wife and me that whenever we walk along a beach where people's bodies are—how shall we say—a bit more exposed than usual, she will inevitably ask me, "Is my butt bigger or smaller than hers?" (This is the only time I give you permission to lie.) Of course, the correct answer is to always point at the other woman, no matter what her shape, and declare with conviction, "Of course yours is smaller!"

I've made it a practice to let Janet know how wonderfully unique she is, incomparable to anyone else. But not every husband handles it that way. Let me tell you the story I heard from a wife's perspective:

Fresh from my shower, I stood in front of the mirror complaining to my husband that my breasts were too small.

Instead of characteristically telling me it's not so, he unchar-acteristically came up with a suggestion.

"If you want them to grow, then every day take a piece of toilet paper and rub it between them for a few seconds."

Willing to try anything, I fetched a piece of toilet paper and stood in front of the mirror, rubbing it between my breasts. "How long will this take?" I asked.

"They will grow larger over a period of years," my hus-band replied.

I stopped. "Do you really think rubbing a piece of toilet paper between them every day will make them larger over the years?"

Without missing a beat he said, "Worked for your butt, didn't it?"

The aftermath to this story is that he's still alive, and with a great deal of therapy, he may even walk again, although he will probably continue to take his meals through a straw. Stupid, stupid man.[48]

We can laugh at this, but it makes the point. When Janet wants to demean herself or apologize that she doesn't look better, I remind her how incredibly sexy I think she is. I thank her for bearing my children and wearing the lifetime battle scars as proof. I take her face in my hands, look longingly in her eyes, and tell her, "Baby, I don't make it a practice to look at naked women anywhere else, so I have nothing to compare you to. For all I know, your body is the epitome of perfection. And I love you just the way you are." Guess how that makes her feel...

Value Her Interests

Observe what's important to your wife. Give attention to learning what she likes. Invest time to help her develop her interests. What makes her tick? What does she enjoy? Compatibility can be learned. When we first got married, we wanted to be with each other all the time. So Janet learned how to shoot baskets and play racquetball. And I learned how to shop for shoes and clothes. To this day, we are best friends and would prefer to be with each other rather than with anyone else.

Now I'm not saying to smother her. It's okay for her to have interests that don't include you. You don't have to tail her to women's "bunko" night or the next home–based Tupperware party. Give her freedom and let her enjoy herself with just her lady friends. I'm simply encouraging you to learn how to be as compatible as possible with her.

MAKE HER FEEL SAFE

"There is nothing nobler or more admirable than when two people who see eye to eye keep house as man and wife, confounding their enemies and delighting their friends."

Homer

There is nothing that makes a woman feel more secure than knowing that her man has things under control. Bring calm to your home.

You can make your wife feel safe and secure in many ways. It should be your objective to do whatever it takes to make her as comfortable as possible. Prove your commitment to the family. Put your immediate family and home before anything or anyone else—especially your extended family: parents, siblings, and other relatives.

Take responsibility for her safety physically, emotionally, relationally, and financially.

PHYSICALLY

Never threaten her physically.

Do I really have to say this? In spite of the obvious anathema, a woman is battered every fifteen seconds within the United States. Statistics reveal that two–thirds of all marriages will experience domestic violence at least once with the man being the abuser ninety–five percent of the time. The largest cause of injury to women is battering—more than car accidents, mugging, and rape combined. Domestic violence is the number–one cause of emergency room visits by women. More than half of battered women stay with their batterer because they do not feel that they can support themselves and their children alone. Over ninety percent of women who killed their husbands had been battered by them.[49]

Ironically, there are even full–blown religions that advocate a husband may beat his wife if she is rebellious or disobedient toward him. Whatever your culture, ethnicity, upbringing, or religious background, there will never be a good enough reason for a husband to physically assault his wife. Your wife is not your property; she is your partner. She should never fear what you might do, so don't even raise your hand to her. Domestic abuse must stop altogether, and it begins by not even making threats. Do what you must to ensure your wife feels safe and protected in your presence.

Protect her from others.

Another way husbands protect their wives is in the unlikely event that someone else should physically hurt their wife. I would expect even the mildest–mannered Clark Kent to rise to the occasion. That doesn't mean you should run out to sign up for classes at the local martial arts center or look to pick a fight just because you think someone looked disrespectfully at your wife. It is simply a confidence vibe you send to your wife that she is in safe hands with you and you would do anything to protect her, even at great personal cost. In the unfortunate event that something should occur, you have a superseding obligation to report it to the authorities and remain within the law. Again, as men we're not looking for opportunities to prove our love to our spouses by inflicting hurt on others. We simply want our girls to know that we would take a bullet for them or run through freeway traffic if it meant saving their life.

Home should be her safe haven.

Let her decorate the home and fix it up the way she wants to. If Erica catches Fred in just the right mood, he will impulsively agree to allow her to redecorate their home. The problem is that his generous feelings vanish all too quickly. When they finally get around to starting the project, he morphs into his tyrannical treasurer alter ego who tightly holds the purse strings, requiring her to submit all suggestions to him for review and final approval. If that wasn't bad enough, Fred then vetoes her selections for new paint colors, questions her fabric choices, and disagrees with her wanting to replace any furniture that is not visibly broken or functionally unusable. Erica is left completely powerless, frustrated, and worse off than if he hadn't agreed in the first place.

A woman's home is her security. It is part of her identity as the place where she can do everything from entertain guests to shelter and cook for her friends and family. Knowing that she spends so much of her time there, a man should allow her the creative autonomy to set up house in a way that's most comfortable for her. Bringing balance to this, I'm not suggesting that the woman should just get to spend and do whatever she wants without marital collaboration. I simply want to encourage the overly involved husband to back off and allow his wife some freedom to enjoy her domain.

Another way to make her home a safe haven is to ensure that the door and window locks to your house are all in working order, perhaps taking it one step further by having a security system installed and dead bolts in place. Let her know how important she is to you by going the extra mile to protect her at home.

Make sure she feels safe in the car.

One of the ways to do this is by taking all the necessary precautions when your wife is away from the house to let her know that you are concerned about her. Make sure she is driving the more dependable vehicle. Will and Kristen had two vehicles in their household. Will had a fairly easy commute. Kristen was a salesperson who had to drive throughout the region all week long. Will drove the newer vehicle, while Kristen was constantly at risk of a smoking engine or a complete automobile breakdown. Men, this is not a very good way to prove your love for your wife.

Consider another couple. Carl and Michelle were the worst to drive together. If Michelle was driving, Carl could not help but to give her play–by–play commentary and advice regarding lane changes and route choices. He would even go so far as to beep the horn for her if he felt she missed the opportunity to do so. Additionally, if Carl was behind the wheel, watch out! He would weave in and out of traffic, using the freeway entrance ramps as an additional available lane to maneuver from whenever possible. He has actually worn out and replaced his horn five times! That has to be a world record. Needless to say, Michelle is extremely uncomfortable going anywhere with Carl and would rather drive separately in order to spare their marriage—as well as her life!

Whether she is driving alone or the two of you are together, the car needs to be a safe place for her. It should be a place where you can have family discussions and enjoyable dialogue. It should not be a frenetic, life–threatening experience for you as well as others on the road.

EMOTIONALLY

Don't talk negatively about her to others.

Like any healthy couple, Brad and Holly don't see eye–to–eye on everything. Welcome to marriage, where two strangers are joined together and expected to live peaceably. However, Brad doesn't like it one bit when Holly will not meekly comply with any of his views or household decisions, as outrageous as they may be. Whether it comes down to disciplining the kids or how to spend money, he is very opinionated on how it should be done and expects her full support. If Holly crosses him, Brad has a unique way of hurting her back. He will call several of his guy friends and, under the pretense of asking their advice, he will totally uncover his wife and spin the story in such a way that she is painted to be a Jezebel and he ends up looking like a saint for even staying with her.

"Don't ever expose your wife's shortcomings."

Don't ever expose your wife's shortcomings. Living your lives together needs to be a mutually safe experience, where mistakes can be made and corrected without the rest of the world looking in all the time. Learn how to peacefully resolve your differences without intentionally hurting her by talking negatively about her to others.

This includes never using her as the butt of your jokes in order to get a laugh from others. Instead, be her buffer. I've been around too many husbands who think it's okay to say things that belittle and degrade their wives. Maybe this makes him feel better about himself. Or perhaps he's punishing her publicly for private indiscretions at home. If he claims this is just innocent fun, then he is poorly trained in the art of relationships. Truth veiled in jest is the coward's way of communicating.

Take her side whenever possible.

Thomas and Brooke recently went for a visit to see Brooke's family. Having a mom and three grown sisters, Brooke is accustomed to the aggressive and boisterous discussions that take place around the kitchen table when everyone is present, and this time would be no different. On this particular occasion, the ladies got into a loud, accusatory debate over how Brooke was mishandling a certain situation. With everyone pointing the finger of blame at her, Brooke became belligerent and assertive in her own defense. Thomas, standing idly nearby, helplessly observed the battle like a spectator at a tennis match watching the ball volleyed from one side to the other.

In the car on the way home, Brooke burst into tears. Thomas, thinking she was crying due to what had just transpired at the mother's house, tried to console her until he realized she was actually crying because of his passive position on the matter. Brooke's topmost complaint was not that her sisters were so mean to her, but that Thomas stood by quietly while her family verbally ravaged her. Our wives need us to be prepared to stand up for them.

Remain committed to her.

When Jack and Carla came into counseling office to see Janet and me, they were emotionally bankrupt. Jack had just been caught having an affair, and while he was willing to come for counseling, he was not sure that he had enough interest to stay in his marriage. The discovery was so recent that Carla was still reeling from her disbelief that it had actually happened. Jack's most bewildering hang-up was wondering what lured him into the affair in the first place. If he really loved Carla, wouldn't he have remained faithful to her? In our office Carla listened to her husband's rhetorical reasoning, the pain on her countenance unmistakable. Not only had he violated her with his infidelity, now his brutal honesty was a frontal emotional assault. She wasn't sure why she had even come for counseling in the first place, knowing that she had every right to walk away from their marriage that he had so blatantly violated.

Any spouse who has lived through the aftermath of an affair knows the pain and havoc it can wreak on your marriage. That's why your wife must know that you are committed to her. She needs to feel safe when it comes to your fidelity, and that includes your emotional faithfulness. To make this point, Janet once told a friend that she could completely trust me even if I were in a room with one hundred naked women. Seizing the moment to compound her compliment with another one, I teasingly added, "I know my wife so well that if you were to put a blindfold on me, I could feel my way around the room and end up identifying which woman was my wife." Let's just say that I should have let her original compliment stand on its own.

But it is true that every woman wants to know that her man only has eyes for her. She needs more than just his promise. She needs to know that her husband won't even take a second look when another pretty lady walks by, regardless of whether or not anyone would even find out. I've always held to the belief that the first look of admiration is free; it's the double–take or bend–your–neck–for–more that will get you in trouble. Your emotional commitment to your wife is a warm blanket on a snowy night keeping her safe and secure.

Remove stressful situations from her.

When I think of the role I play in my marriage, I recognize my responsibility to reduce Janet's stress provokers whenever plausible. By doing so, I can accomplish a couple of goals. For starters, she perceives me as this hero who has stepped in to rescue her, and then she becomes eternally grateful toward me. Additionally, I allow her to preserve her physical and emotional strength so that she can function at a greater capacity for the tasks she is still required to tackle.

Husbands have the unique privilege of protecting their wives from any number of uncomfortable or difficult situations if they would only be willing to step up and do so. Some of the diverse imaginable scenarios include, but are not limited to, administering discipline to the children; averting confrontation when someone is rude or unprofessional; handling awkward interactions like merchandise exchanges; and intercepting unpleasant phone calls as in the case of bill collectors or your child's schoolteacher.

When the neighbor called our house screaming and complaining that our son had broken their truck window, Janet was caught off guard, a bit flustered, and at a loss for words. Seeing her dismay, I quickly reacted by asking if I could take the phone from her. She immediately acquiesced, allowing me to inquire further about the situation. Diplomatically, I interceded on my wife's behalf, allowing the neighbor to vent and relate their side of the story uninterrupted. I promised to get to the bottom of it with my son and resolve the matter swiftly for the neighbor.

Your involvement is not intended to imply that women are weak or can't handle these situations even better than men. Often they could, and, even more frequently, they should. I am simply trying to put men on alert as to how they can become champions for their wives if their ladies will allow them to.

RELATIONALLY

Guard her from negative relationships that would otherwise eat away at her. These relationships can be in the form of your parents, her parents, ex–spouse, boss, friend, sibling, coworker—basically, anyone who attempts to push the envelope too far.

Choose friendships wisely.

Choose your friends wisely. Just because you grew up with someone does not mean that safeguarding that friendship is healthy for your marriage. Sometimes the best decision is to move on, if not altogether, than at least with some clearly defined boundaries.

Limit friendships outside your gender. I've heard females say, "But I just get along better with the guys." And that may be true, but after marriage your devotion is to your one man.

Rick and Linda were best friends with Jeff and Amanda. On top of that, both couples had children all around the same ages. They were known to share family vacations and holiday get–togethers. When Jeff and Amanda got divorced, Jeff found himself not only blindsided, but also a bit jaded on life. Not willing to leave their friend out in the cold, Rick and Linda continued to invite Jeff along with them, even when the kids were not involved. Over the course of time, Linda's compassion toward Jeff's unfortunate circumstances turned into a passion for him as the two then ended up in an extramarital affair. Now the moral of the story is not to leave your opposite–gender friends high and dry in times of turmoil, but to set some boundaries and accountabilities to ensure you protect the sanctity of your own marriage.

Guard your outside relationships and interests.

Outside interests for marriage partners are certainly acceptable when balanced. It is paramount that you are both in agreement as to the terms and guidelines of those pleasures. Whether it's girls' night out, tennis doubles, poker night, or men's bowling league, make sure that each other is okay with the arrangements. And if at all possible, support each other's leisure activities. Cheer on his softball games. Invite her to your tennis matches. Let her bring her cheerleading pom–poms to your golf match play. (Only kidding…There are limits before it just gets weird.) Stay involved in as many aspects of each other's lives so that you don't grow apart. And, of course, don't smother one another. Give her space to enjoy her girls' night out. I wouldn't expect to see you sitting at the card table during her ladies' bridge night. Stay interested in each other's interests.

More than all the aforementioned independent activities, enjoy your time with one another, since you never know how much time you will ultimately have together. Whatever you do together, do it like you might never get to do it again. Enjoy your morning coffee while watching the sunrise. Make road trips a fun way to grow closer by getting to know more about each other. Whether shopping for groceries or holiday gifts, count your blessings that you are even able to do so, and do it with joy. Be fun to be around so that you are her favorite person to spend time with.

When it comes to hanging out with others, who you spend your time with determines how far you will go in life. So choose your outside relationships wisely and strategically. And don't be the lone ranger who makes social decisions without consulting your wife. Collaboratively agree on the who, what, and where. Phil and Faye had been married for over twenty–five years. Phil's habit was to invite people over without giving Faye any fair warning. To be completely honest, Faye did not have a say. It was Phil's agenda, and he just expected Faye to abide by it. Although Phil did not expect his wife to do anything in way of preparation for his impromptu guests, Faye still felt like the condition of the house and preparation of foods were a reflection on her, so she always ended up working anyway.

Protect her from manipulative children.

Shield her from the children when necessary. As awesome as they might be, kids can also be master manipulators. In our home we never let children come between us or play one parent against the other. Whenever one of my children approached me and made a request, my first response was always, "What did your mother say?" That way I knew which angle they were coming from. If Janet had already consented by saying, "It's all right with me, but check with your father," then I recognized she was simply looking for a supporting vote or final verdict on the matter, and I had to be willing to be that decision maker. I always wanted to make certain that my response would be in concert with hers, or if I disagreed with her position, it would not be evident to the children but could be discussed privately later. But if she had already refused their request, barring special circumstances, the children were not permitted to come to me and ask again. Doing so would always result in consequences.

Solidarity is the key to successful parenting. Your children have to see Mom and Dad on the same page. In eighteen years they will be gone, but you will still have a lifetime of marriage ahead of you. Do you have enough invested in your relationship to persevere to the finish line?

Raising children of your own has enough challenges. But consider two divorcees who marry, both bringing their own children into the relationship, and now you have a potentially even more volatile setting. What started out for Gary and Kara as two hurt individuals getting a second chance at love became the reality of blending two families and asking the children to merge histories and share parents. Kara's teenaged children didn't want to take any instruction from Gary. After all, they said, "He's not my father." And Gary's kids had emotionally checked out and withdrawn themselves from their new stepfamily altogether. Whenever the children are given responsibilities from their stepparent that they don't agree with, they simply whine to their natural parent and plead for advocacy. Thankfully, Gary saw this manipulation for what it was and called a family meeting to establish new boundaries and release Kara from feeling like she had to play their rescuer.

"In a marriage you're promising to care about everything. The good things, the bad things, the terrible things, the mundane things…all of it, all of the time, every day. You're saying 'Your life will not go unnoticed because I will notice it. Your life will not go un-witnessed because I will be your witness.'"

Susan Sarandon, from the movie
Shall We Dance

Buffer her from extended family.

Never tell your parents all the bad stuff about your spouse (unless you need protection or intervention). While you forgive and forget, your parents will never forget and may be prone to holding grudges. Soon you will be wondering why your parents are unkind to your mate or why your in–laws are acting funny toward you. Well, it's obvious…You both have been blabbing to your parents about each other. You've heard the cliché "What happens in Vegas, stays in Vegas." I'm not entirely suggesting that your marriage be treated with the same sense of absolute privacy, but there is some wisdom in carefully selecting what should be made public and what should be worked out privately. Because once it's worked out, others didn't need to be exposed to your dirty laundry.

Protect her from your family. Harry and Amelia were very close friends of ours, married for over fifteen years. Because Amelia worked outside the home, she often needed assistance to pick up the kids from school or rush them to ball practice. If Harry was not available, he would typically turn to the most common sense solution: his mom or sister. After all, his parents and sister really loved Harry's children and genuinely enjoyed helping out while spending quality time with the kids. Although Amelia welcomed their help and acknowledged her in–laws' kindness and support for the children, Amelia somehow was always made to feel like the outsider. Perhaps it was her own paranoia or insecurities, but the in–laws had a way of taking over and doing more than what was asked from them. To most that would mean welcome relief. To Amelia it sent the subtle, subliminal message that they could care for the children better than Amelia, undermining her maternal role.

There would be times when Amelia would return home from an exhausting day's work only to have her kitchen cabinets randomly rearranged by her mother–in–law. Another time Harry's mom took their daughter for a haircut without consulting with either one of the parents simply because Grandma thought the child needed it. The mother–in–law would frequently pack the children's overnight bag and then let Amelia know about it later, after the plans were already put in motion with the children. If Amelia vetoed the plans, she was the party pooper accused of ruining her children's weekend.

Whether or not the mother–in–law's intentions were to be purely helpful or deviously controlling, Amelia did not appreciate the intrusion whatsoever. Amelia grew to resent her in–laws yet felt like she was between a rock and a hard place. She desperately needed the assistance that her in–laws lovingly offered but did not appreciate the emotional price she felt forced to pay.

On several occasions Amelia clearly communicated her feelings to Harry and implored him to intervene on her behalf. He would quickly dismiss her entreaties and remind Amelia how lost they would be without his family's help and that she should learn to show more appreciation.

Amelia did not want to forfeit her in-laws' involvement altogether; she just desperately wanted Harry to help clarify the boundaries. Harry would rather have played goalie for an archery team than stand up to the archetypal matriarchs of his lineage. This struggle compounded the stress already pressuring the fault line of their relationship. I'm sorry to report that their marriage succumbed to divorce.

If you ever have to choose between your wife and your parents, always choose your wife. It is a God-given directive to let your wife know that she comes first in your life and that you're not still holding onto your childhood relationship.

Justin and Donna were not married that long. Donna's mother was recovering from cancer and living on governmental assistance. Because of her mother's pathetic lot in life, Donna felt very responsible for her well-being. Although her compassion may seem admirable to an outsider, Donna began ignoring her husband's pleas for attention and placed her mom's situation ahead of her marriage. Even while subsisting on meager finances to support their household, Donna would take money from their own obligations to help her mom. This eventually became the ruin of their marriage, as Justin now felt he came in second place, and Donna felt that Justin did not understand or care about her mother's plight. What Justin did perceive was that his mother-in-law was manipulative and always on the take, and he resented that his wife played right into her schemes. Best as he could, Justin tried to help Donna see things more objectively, but Donna was blinded by her self–imposed familial obligations and considered Justin's pleas nothing more than immature, calloused jealousy. Because they both felt justified with their behavior and unwilling to go to counseling or see the other's view, their short marriage ended in divorce.

FINANCIALLY

Work hard for your family.

A woman needs to feel financially secure, and husbands should accept their responsibility to guarantee that security. I happen to know firsthand that this can be easier said than done. Today, many households have two income earners, with the wife frequently earning more than the husband. For that reason, some families have made the conscious decision that the wife serve as primary bread-winner while the husband stay at home and tend to the children. This area can have a sundry of possibilities. Bottom line: Assuring that your family has enough money lies on your shoulders as much as it's within your power to do something about it.

Entrepreneurial pursuits are acceptable so long as you and your wife have calculated the costs—both financial and emotional—and understand the associated risks. James is a contractor. He performs residential renovations and basement build–outs. Competition has intensified, the economy has shifted, and profitability margins have been reduced. Now what was once a strong business is no longer producing enough income to sustain the family. Melissa is very stressed and has asked James to reconsider his employment options. She would like for him to go back to his old job within the electrical union where they will be guaranteed work and a set wage, or if he is adamant on keeping his business open, at least consider taking on an additional part–time position until the market shifts again. James and Melissa have fought furiously over this issue. He thinks that Melissa doesn't believe in him and interprets that as a personal blow to his ego. Here's the rub…James has made the error of only thinking about his side of the situation and not understanding Melissa's vantage point. As a woman, she has an innate need for security and is beginning to feel vulnerable as she imagines her domestic situation spiraling out of control.

Although we all wish for a lifetime of prosperity and ease, there is a strong reality that you will have challenges in this area. It may be due to the lack of money or the different styles of management (or lack thereof) within the household. Or, as hard as it is to believe, too much money can also be a noose around one's neck if the proper precautions are not taken. I know what you're thinking…*Give me a chance to try that for myself, and I'll let you know.* But if that were not the case, then the divorce rate among the affluent would be statistically distinct from other socio-economic classes. Don't ever let your finances bring stress to your marriage. Work as a team.

It reminds me of the guy who asked his wife, "Do you love me just because my father left me a fortune?" She replied, "Not at all, honey; I would love you no matter who left you the money."[50]

Honor your wife's need for financial security by being a hard worker. Whether you sit in the office of a metropolitan high–rise, deliver the mail door–to–door, serve by teaching in the public school system, or explore and excavate the underground tunnels of our city's sewers, take pride in your work and do it for the betterment of your family.

Don't put your family in debt.

Men often tease how women love to shop. Whether bargain hunting or window–shopping, the question of need is often irrelevant, as most women just enjoy the experience itself.

Brian cannot understand Cathy's fixation on jewelry. He rationalizes that you can only wear one wristwatch at a time, so why bother owning more than one. In his mind the same logic applies to rings, bracelets, earrings, and the rest. According to him, anything left over in her jewelry box is just a frivolous waste of money that could have been better used elsewhere. Truth be told, however, while men may not be naturally inclined to shop, they are still the ones who cause most of the financial damage to the household because of their obsession with expensive and impulsive purchases. It's the man who typically buys the home theater with surround sound along with the 84" plasma television, or the brand new luxury car with all the bells and whistles. For a man, these purchases define his perceived level of success, and, therefore, he becomes gripped by them.

Don't be a squanderer. Try to understand your wife's need to take care of herself by getting her manicures and pedicures, having her hair highlighted, or using the tanning bed. At the same time, it's okay for you to enjoy the little pleasures life offers as well. Just make sure that those expenditures are budgeted for and fairly distributed.

HE NEVER TALKS TO ME ...

"The goal in marriage is not to think alike, but to think together."

Robert C. Dodds

Much of your success in life depends on your ability to relate and interact with others. And your capacity to do this depends on how well you have honed your communication skills.

Think about a job interview. A skilled interviewer typically begins the interview with some form of an icebreaker to ease the tension: "How was your drive in today?" or, "Did you find our office okay?" The interviewer is attempting to relax you by eliminating any awkward tension caused by the unpredictability of your new surroundings. After the interviewer warms you up a bit, they then proceed to the meat–and–potatoes of the Q&A session.

"Tell me about yourself."

"Why do you want to work for our company?"

"Where do you see yourself in the next five years?"

Your ability to effectively field those questions and volley back well–thought–out, pointed responses will determine whether or not the interviewer concludes you are worthy of further consideration and possibly a good fit for the role. Can you imagine an interviewee not answering the questions but just sitting there with a blank stare? Or what if the only answers given were grunts, yes/no, "I don't know," or, worst of all, silence? A person's inability to respond intelligently and refusal to actively participate in a discussion makes all the difference in how well that person is perceived. It is also an indictment on that person's interest level to embrace the opportunity to relate with the speaker.

If you are willing to make intentional efforts to communicate in the workplace in order to gain or maintain your employment, then decide to implement that very same practice at home. Our spouses, whom we have vowed to spend a lifetime with, have the same right to our honest and open conversations that we give our employers and clients.

WHAT COMMUNICATION IS

Communication is freedom of expression. Within the framework of marriage, communication should offer the permission to express oneself without risk of ridicule, judgment, or reprisal. In a healthy marriage, each partner should be able to say whatever is on their mind while using a common sense filter of basic etiquette. In other words, no one should deliberately voice mean–spirited insults or slanderous accusations with the malicious objective of hurting the other. It is not appropriate to act that way at school, work, or church; don't do it at home. Freedom of speech within marriage is liberating to the individuals and bonding for the couple. It sets a healthy environment for open exchange to understand each other's viewpoints, clarify issues, reconcile differences, organize together, plan for the future, and share everyday experiences.

There are some right and wrong ways to do this. Nick and Carrie have been married for more than twenty years. They spend a lot of time talking to one another; however, it always includes derision and sarcasm administered at elevated decibels. Nothing is ever discussed civilly. What starts out as normal conversation seems to always end up in a blowout–shouting match. When Nick wanted to hire another person to help out in the family business, Carrie was obviously not in agreement. She called him everything from lazy to ignorant regarding how to run the operation. She knows how to push Nick's buttons so that he gets mad enough to the point of exasperation. And she will do this in front of their children. Once he explodes, she then further belittles him by exposing to the kids how their dad can't control his temper. This causes him to withdraw and relent. Do you think Nick will initiate future discussions like this one with Carrie?

Compare that to Tom and Sophia. Sophia's elderly parents have asked to come for a two-week visit over the holidays. Sophia's mom is very negative and opinionated; you always know when she's in the room because you no longer want to be there. She never lifts a finger and expects to be waited on hand and foot, and she expects to be treated to any and all family outings. Tension presides in their home during these perennial visits, and the family can hardly wait for their guests' departure so that order can be restored. Upon hearing of his in-laws' plans to visit, Tom beckoned to Sophia.

"We've got to talk."

"What's up?" she inquired, pretending not to know what was on his agenda.

"Two weeks, Sophia?" he began. "Your parents want to come visit for two weeks? They know our place is small and the kids will have to give up their bedrooms."

"Tom, this makes me very uncomfortable," she responded. "I feel like I'm in a lose-lose predicament. If I leave things as is, then you're unhappy with me. But if I address it with my parents, then they will feel hurt and think we don't want them here. What do you expect me to do?"

"I know, sweetie," Tom continued. "I'm sorry to make you feel like that. You know I love your parents. It's just that I wish I could love them for one week instead of two. Aren't there any other possibilities?"

"If there were, Tom, you know I would already have suggested it. I'm afraid we're just going to have to deal with this and make the best of it."

Tom relented. "You're right. We'll get through, and we'll even have a good time…We always do."

A husband's ability to effectively communicate within his marriage is essential to the success of his relationship. Obviously, he needs a wife who is safe to talk to and willing to accept responsibility for her end of the discussion. Be that as it may, audibly speaking what is on your heart and mind ensures that your wife will not misinterpret what you are thinking. Your conversation reveals your heart because words are typically an overflow of what is stored inside. So make time and effort to relax and enjoy meaningful conversation with your wife.

There are several advantages to healthy communication within your marriage. Stop saying, "I'm a guy and just don't feel like talking." The choice is yours. You have the power to take your relationship to the next level by incorporating just a few tips on how to have more meaningful conversation with your wife.

Enjoy Small Talk

As superficial as small talk may seem, it's an essential part of a couple's communication regimen. I'm always amused and refreshed by young love. When a couple is getting to know one another, they spend all their waking time talking to each other, whether over the phone or over a cup of coffee. It's at this information–gathering stage where they develop a ravenous appetite to learn as much as possible about the other's interests, family composition, career aspirations, background, future plans, favorite foods, dreams, and much, much more.

Whenever we see new couples in our office for premarital counseling sessions, we ask these couples to individually respond to some of the most random questions:

- What about your own childhood do you want to be different for your children?

- What possessions or items would you grab if your house was on fire?

- Besides marriage and children, what is something significant you want to accomplish in life?

What's so interesting is not only listening to the individual read their answer aloud, but watching the partner assimilate that response. A lot of times this is new information that the couple has not discussed before, so each person is taking mental notes. The responses usually generate some lively and positive discussion as each person is learning something new about their mate–to–be.

Here's the rub…In too many relationships there comes a mystifying point in time where one or both participants grow weary of learning about their partner. It's not planned; it just happens. Conversation becomes a chore, and the easy way out is to avoid it. The mystique surrounding your partner is no longer as intriguing as it once was, so not worth the effort of exploring. Don't let that happen. Fight on through. Don't take for granted that you already know everything. Like taste buds that can change over time, likes and dislikes can fluctuate as well. You should make it your goal to enjoy a lifetime of conversing with one another and learning everything you can about each other.

Express Your Love

It's one thing to love your wife. It's another to verbalize it in a way that she can hear it. Say "I love you" to her every day, preferably several times a day. Don't ever assume that she should already know you love her. Hearing those magical words brings a sense of security and assurance. There are so many lonely, hurting people in this world who don't have someone to adore and affirm them. Don't take your situation for granted. Appreciate it by appreciating her. Tell her how much you love her and do so sincerely.

It's like the story about the man who, when questioned about his love for his wife, stated, "I told her I loved her when we got married. Why do I need to say it again? If anything changes, I'll let her know."[51] Amusing as that may be, how many people do we know who seem to live out their marriage like that?

"If you love someone you say it, you say it right then, out loud. Otherwise the moment just...passes you by."

Dermot Mulroney, from the movie
My Best Friend's Wedding

My friend Steve amazes me the way he always finds a way to say something flowery and poetic about his wife. He refers to her as though she were royalty: "Lady Bonnie." To hear him speak, you would imagine her to be the most beautiful and important female dignitary in the world. She is quite attractive, but that's beside the point. Steve is quick to place her on his pedestal for public viewing. Not only does he tell her how much he loves her, but he often does it while others are around. How do you think this makes her feel? Invincible, I'm sure!

Be quick to let her know that you love her. Life is full of so many unpredictable turns in the road that it is not worth the risk of waiting until tomorrow if you have opportunity to tell her today.

Strive to Understand and Be Understood

Make sure you communicate clearly. When Shannon was going through a rough patch, Isaac decided to send her a flower bouquet to help pick her up. He called the florist, made arrangements for delivery, and dictated his message of affirmation: "I believe in you."

When he returned home later that day, he could tell that Shannon had been crying. Seeing the beautiful bouquet on the table, he inquired, "How did you like the flowers?"

She burst into tears. "With all I'm going through, this is how you break the news?"

Completely bewildered, Isaac recalled sending the message "I believe in you." He walked over to the flowers and read the card transcribed by the florist. It said, "I be leaving you."[52]

Simple dialogue can help clear the air when misunderstandings try to form and take root. By nicely airing your thoughts, you give legitimacy to your feelings so that your partner can better relate to you and understand what's going on. Since neither one of you are mind readers, you need to let her into your heart and mind. Fostering a spirit of understanding in your relationship lets the other person know that their feelings are valid as well as important to you. What a privilege it can be to share life with another person when you both are trying to understand one another and do what's best for the other.

Plan Your Future

One of the most valuable times I have to learn more about Janet is when we take time to dream and plan our future together. While some of it may really be nothing more than daydreaming or fantasizing, it still provides me insights into her soul concerning what is important to her.

We may be going for a walk holding hands or sipping a cup of coffee at a sidewalk café and I'll start asking her questions:

- If you could visit any place in the world, where would it be?

- What would be your perfect vacation home setting?

- How would you describe the perfect retirement?

- If you won the lottery, what would you do with the money?

- If money weren't an issue, what would you do with your life?

Knowing her as well as I do, some of her responses are fairly predictable, while others catch me by surprise and give us a chance to intimately discuss our future. It's a good reminder that I shouldn't take for granted that I already know all there is to know about her.

So try it. Turn the TV off and put the kids to bed. Lay her head in your lap, stroke her hair, and just share your dreams with one another. Take one of these questions—or make up one of your own—and put it out there for discussion. This will provide a deeper connection with her while ensuring that you not grow apart but maintain an emotional connection with one another.

Rehearse Your History

Reminiscing over our past mutual experiences is one of the most cherished times a couple can share. Of course, I mean our positive experiences. There is something very magical and romantic when you recall what attracted you to each other in the first place, or how you first met, or where you went on a first date. Whenever I counsel with a couple that seems to be on the brink of breakup, I try to maneuver the discussion to get them to talk about what they first liked about each other. Even if just for a brief moment, you can see the transformation begin on their countenance as a deluge of positive memories seems to flood their memory banks.

Don't wait until a marriage counselor has to push you in this direction. Make it your practice to rehearse your history. While mature love is very strong and distinctive, there is something special about remembering when love was new and all the physiological effects it brought.

Find a place and time to do this sooner than later. Keep the experience fresh in your memories.

WHAT COMMUNICATION IS *NOT*

Inasmuch as you can speak life and motivation into your wife, your words are powerful enough to become a destructive wedge in your marriage as well. Think about all the thoughtless comments husbands have made to their wives:

- "Trust me…It's not the dress that's making you look fat."

- "Did you mean for dinner to taste like that?"

- "How come you don't look like so–and–so?"

- "My mother didn't fold my laundry like that."

- "Is our anniversary on the sixteenth or the nineteenth?"

- "I'm not making the bed. That's your job."

- "Do you mind if I leave the game on while we make love?"

Just one misguided five–second utterance has enough potency to destroy the peace in your relationship for the rest of the day. Take time to think about her feelings before you callously blurt out something.

Once you are attempting to communicate with your wife in order to go to a deeper level of emotional intimacy, avoid the most common conversation killers. Although these should be obvious to all, beginners and veterans alike, here is a list of blatant no–nos to avoid:

- *Screaming.* There is never a good reason to shout and yell at someone—especially your wife. Show me an instance when this has produced the desired results for both parties. Either you end up alienating one another or one wins and the other loses miserably. Learn how to have civil discussions without raising your voice. You can do it in the business world; do it at home.

- *Comparisons.* Comparing her to someone else's wife as a way to point out her inadequacies or deficiencies is a sure way to violate trust with her. Moreover, it sends the message to her that you might be more interested in this other woman that you seem to know so much about. Just because another woman appears to have certain desirable positive traits, it doesn't mean she would do well as your wife. It's probably due to the fact that her husband is bringing out the best in her so that those positive traits shine. So tend to your own garden by giving it the proper loving care and you'll be surprised at the great results you can help produce in your woman.

- *Criticism.* Hurling insults is not only demeaning and condescending, it is also very hurtful to her psyche. These will have long–lasting negative effects even after the battle is over. Be careful what you say. The words of your mouth have the ability to give life and refreshing to your wife or bring death to your relationship. Think about that the next time you want to criticize her. Do you want to be married to the walking dead?

- *Excuses.* Until you can take responsibility for your own actions and reactions, your relationship will never progress beyond its current condition. When dialoging with your wife over differences, learn to man up and accept your part in the conflict. Stop making excuses or you will never move forward.

- *Profanity.* Name-calling and swear words seem to become the weapons of choice for so many couples during a fight, but that doesn't make it right or even close to acceptable. Using profanity just lowers the standard that much more and makes you look like a lowlife. If you wouldn't want your children to repeat your words, then don't use them in the first place. Furthermore, if you wouldn't tolerate another man speaking to your wife that way, what gives you the right?

- *Dredging up the past.* Dwelling on former mistakes is an unfair strategy when conversing with her. Just like you would want your past improprieties forgiven and forgotten, do the same for her. If you can never get beyond the mistakes of her past, how will you navigate successfully here in the present or in the future? Your wife has to know that apologies and forgiveness may not be able to erase a memory, but it's often the best we can offer, so let it be good enough to move on from.

- *Threats.* Your wife should never have her life or her security threatened by you. Don't take a dictatorial posture where it has to be your way or the highway. Only a bully and a coward would employ these tactics to intimidate his wife. And then you wonder why you don't have a good marriage. You don't deserve one!

- *Silent treatment.* Using the silent treatment may have been a popular ploy in middle school to get back at someone, but it's time to grow up. While you might have to give each other some time and space to cool down, be mature enough to finish what you started without ignoring one another.

HOW TO DEVELOP YOUR COMMUNICATION

Realize She Needs It

Remember, if it's important to her, it's important—because women, by nature, need to talk. If you as her husband are not willing or available to meet that need, she will find someone else to talk to—maybe it's her girlfriend or that male co-worker who sits in the next cubicle. Don't relinquish your emotional attachment with your wife to someone else, because once she turns that corner, it may be hard to get her back.

"If it's important to her, it's important."

One of the biggest complaints I've heard from women through the years is about their husband's inability to communicate or plain unwillingness to try. We all have a free will on this one. And admittedly, some people like talking more than others. Generally speaking, the female gender is a bit more prone to chattiness than her male counterpart. It is common knowledge that women like to speak nearly twice as much as men. Likewise, most of their words are reserved for their home setting especially as in the case of the stay–at–home mom, whereas men typically exhaust the majority of their conversational needs in the workplace, so by the time they return home, they may be completely spent. Regardless of the logic, be there for her and be willing to spend some quality time talking and listening.

Include Her in Your Life

When a woman says, "He never talks to me…" she is usually complaining that her husband seems unwilling to express his feelings or to let her into his world. This could be as simple as the following exchange:

Wife: "How was work today, honey?"

Husband: "Good."

Wife: "Anything new and exciting happen?"

Husband: "No."

Although the husband has politely answered his wife's questions, she is left feeling ostracized. Now she's angry with or hurt by him, and he is left feeling perplexed since, according to his standards, he answered all her questions. Instead, what she is looking for is inclusion. She wants to feel like an insider. She does not need a complete run-down of the day's activities, just enough highlights to help her relate to her husband's situation. Check out a similar dialogue.

Wife: "How was work today, honey?"

Husband: "Actually, pretty good. The day seemed to fly by."

Wife: "Oh, that's good. Anything new and exciting happen?"

Husband: "Not really. It's just that Jason Parker mentioned he might be taking over the Southeast division, and that would vacate another opening on our team."

Wife: "Who would take over his spot?"

Husband: "That's the interesting part. Management seems pretty tight–lipped. They must be up to something."

Communication lets your wife know she's valuable. With a slight tweaking of the husband's responses and the insertion of some specific news, the wife now feels like his partner and confidant. Just a little corporate chatter and these spouses have now paved additional common ground for further discussion. Like a soap opera junkie, she becomes riveted to this real–life drama, and you can be sure she will be checking on its progress in the ensuing days.

Show Interest in Her Life

At the same time, it is important to show genuine interest in your wife's day. Continuing the conversation:

Husband: "And how about you, sweetheart…How was your day today?"

Wife: "Nothing unusual. Anthony was running late, so I dropped him at school. I took Emily for a playdate at the park, visited Aunt Sarah in the nursing home, went grocery shopping, and then started on dinner."

Husband: "About Aunt Sarah…How's she doing?"

Wife: "The same. You know Aunt Sarah…She's a feisty one. Always manages to keep the staff on their toes."

Husband: "Have I told you how much I appreciate you? You really amaze me with all you can do."

Wife: "Aww…You're so sweet."

When you exhibit a sincere interest in your wife, you're telling her how important she is to you. Just a few moments of dialog about her day lets her know that you are genuinely concerned about her well–being.

Find Things to Talk About

Just because a husband and wife have conversations does not mean the quality and content of their discussions passes muster. Take Larry and Marge, for example. They like to have sit–down discussions. As a matter of fact, Larry, unlike most of his male counterparts, is unchar-acteristically the one who usually initiates the need for dialogue. Their agenda can be anything from disciplining the children to managing the household budget. While it sounds like Larry has his act together regarding communication, there are typically some underlying motives to his meetings. Truth be told, he is not looking to have any friendly banter over the topics at hand. Larry wants a captive audience where he can lay down the law about what has not worked and how his new directives will help solve the problem. For Larry, Marge is not there to participate, but to agree with his newly formulated dictatorial platform—again.

So don't take pride if you are the kind of guy who takes time to talk to your wife. There is more to effective communication than dominating demands. There are so many things that need to be discussed within the context of marriage from household responsibilities to money matters to upcoming events. Stay connected with her so that she has a partner who enhances her life and makes things easier.

COMPLIMENT HER ...
OR SOMEONE ELSE WILL

"Try praising your wife, even if it does frighten her at first."

Billy Sunday

A husband and wife were comparing notes one day.

"I have a higher IQ, did better on my SATs, and make more money than you," she pointed out.

"Yeah, but when you step back and look at the big picture, I'm still ahead," he said.

She looked baffled. "How do you figure?"

"I married better," he replied.[53]

Nice job, buddy. Way to turn it back around. Paying a sincere compliment has many benefits. You are able to convey your admiration, appreciation, and affirmation while inspiring her to higher heights as a person. In addition, you, too, will be refreshed for choosing to offer your wife the gift of life–giving words.

ADMIRE HER

There is always something good that can be said about your wife. It is like the husband and wife who were getting ready for bed. The wife was standing in front of a full–length mirror, taking a hard look at herself.

"You know, dear," she says, "I look in the mirror, and I see an old woman. My face is all wrinkled, my hair is gray, my shoulders are hunched over, I've got fat legs, and my arms are all flabby." She turns to her husband and says, "Tell me something positive to make me feel better about myself."

He studies hard for a moment, thinking about it, and then says in a soft, thoughtful voice, "Well, there's nothing wrong with your eyesight."[54]

Part of communication is verbally affirming your wife. Always be quick to compliment your spouse. If you don't, someone else will. As human beings, we relish affirmation and encouragement. Compliments cause us to soar above our situation. I know, for me, if you tell me that I look good or did something well, then you have catapulted me to the top of the mountain, where I can conquer anything. I become invincible. So praise your wife. Commend her cooking, her intellect, the way she dotes over your children, her job skills, her kindness, whatever you can think of. And trust me; she has lots of noteworthy traits if you will just take the time to treasure hunt her many gifts. Even if others recognize her uniqueness, always make sure those sentiments come first and foremost from you, so that when given by another, their impact pales in comparison.

"You make me want to be a better man."

Jack Nicholson, from the movie
As Good As It Gets

My wife is incredible. Not only is she extremely talented and caring, she is also very beautiful to look at. I have made it a practice early in our marriage to notice what she is wearing or how she has fixed her hair. I'll comment on the coordination of her outfit, or the way she has done her makeup. I make sure I tell her how phenomenal she looks and how I could just stare at her all day. I'll find something to say about the color of her eyes, or her cute little nose, or how the smell of her perfume drives me wild. I make sure she unequivocally knows that she is desired by me. (I'll leave that to your imagination.) After we kiss, she is quick to tell me that she has left lipstick imprints on my lips or cheek and that I should wipe it off. I playfully tease her by telling her that I like those marks because it is a sign to the world of our intimacy and that I belong to her. Her eyes twinkle at those remarks.

Throughout the years, Janet has had plenty of men pay her attention and even go so far as to tell her that she looks good. But guess what? She's already fulfilled by the admiring gazes and sexually charged looks I have been steadily giving her. I've already told her multiple times how incredible she looks and how blessed I am to call her my wife. So while it may be momentarily flattering to hear it from others, it is only a faint echo compared to what she hears from me all the time.

Starve your puppy and eventually she will go looking for scraps anywhere she can find them. She might climb onto the kitchen table or even wander over to the neighbor's yard to check out what's in that dog's bowl. If you had the dog food to feed your puppy, then why wouldn't you do it? So it is with human nature. You deprive your wife of your compliments long enough and she becomes vulnerable to the attention of another. It doesn't justify, nor does it guarantee that she will take that route, but why deprive her of the verbal attention she needs?

Dr. Hook sang a song back in the 1970s entitled "When You're In Love with a Beautiful Woman."[55] He sings about everybody hitting on your girl because of her beauty. He alleges that if you don't watch closely, she may even end up in your closest friend's arms. If that's the case, who would want to marry a beautiful woman?

I can tell through firsthand experience that being married to a beautiful woman can be undeniably wonderful. The compliments I speak to my wife are not birthed out of insecurity that if I don't do it, she will go looking elsewhere. Rather, it is my honor to make her feel that special, as though she is the most incredible woman in the world because that's the way I actually see it. After practicing it for a while, those compliments actually flow much easier now. So when she leaves the house and some stranger in the supermarket or office tells her that she looks pretty, how do you think she takes it? Well, of course, like any normal person she feels flattered. But at least she is not overly impressed or stirred by these empty words. Like a well–nourished puppy, she is completely satisfied. She is already secure in her husband and lover at home.

One of the greatest examples of this has been exhibited by Pastor Jim. Time and again he has stood in the pulpit of our large congregation and found a way to incorporate into his sermon some positive attributes regarding his wife, Robin, which he will publicly proclaim. He refers to her as his best friend. With his unique self–deprecating style of humor, he relates how much she has had to put up with through the years having him for a husband. And he declares how many times he would have cut and run from his pressure–filled profession if he did not have the strength and support of a cheering partner behind him. Having known Pastor Jim for more than seventeen years—on both a public platform as well as through private friendship—I can assuredly state that he is one hundred percent genuine, and I have never heard him speak anything negative about his wife. By the way, we love Robin too.

ACKNOWLEDGE HER

Give credit to whom credit is due—especially when it comes to your wife. Too many husbands like to blame their wives when something goes wrong, but they're quick to take the credit when things go well. It has been my experience that a woman simply wants to be recognized for the contributions she makes to the marriage and the family.

> "Give credit to whom credit is due—
> especially when it comes to your wife."

Lauren works in the local school system. Her husband, Norm, works very hard at his own business of building and restoring furniture. As a self-employed entrepreneur, his only access to family health insurance is what he is willing to pay for. Part of the family strategy was for Lauren to take on this job so they can all benefit by the school's insurance coverage. A simple acknowledgment from Norm letting Lauren know how thankful he is for her selfless efforts on the family's behalf was all the kudos she needed to keep her going.

While it's very important to give your woman a steady diet of praise, make sure your children are able to participate in the fun. How many times have I handed out some corny pick-up line to my wife. My kids would roll their eyes or playfully scoff at it, all the while totally relishing the moment and the impact it had on Janet. I remember the time we drove into the country to a dog breeder who was raising Great Pyrenees, a beautiful large breed of dog originally used for protecting livestock. I told the kids that the last time I saw a "great pair–of–knees" was when their mom got out of the shower this morning. Of course, they all teasingly groan and mock my humor, but deep down they love when I lavish their mom with compliments.

I've always been quick to thank my wife in front of the children for her commitment to our family, telling her how great the house looks and what a superb meal she has prepared. They have even heard me tell her that I can't believe how fortunate I am to have her for my wife. That steady diet of acknowledgment lets Janet know how much I love and value her. If I'm going to require my children to value their mom, then I must lead the charge. There have been many times when I've asked one of my sons, "Did you see Mom today? Don't you think she looks especially beautiful?" Whether or not they truly think so or simply feel cornered by my questioning, they invariably respond, "Yeah, she does." Then I go for the kill. "Well, did you tell her yet? She can't guess what you are thinking until you let her know." I'll see my son sheepishly walk into the next room and say, "Hey, Mom, you look really nice today." She glows, and I gloat even more. Or I might ask them, "How did you like dinner tonight, guys?" They answer, "It was really good." So I'll follow up with, "Did you let your mom know how great it was and how much you appreciate her taking her time to prepare it for you? There were lots of other things she could have done with her time instead of waiting on us." My sons follow through, and meanwhile they have learned a priceless lesson to carry into their marriages.

In addition to recognizing her accomplishments and abilities, it is important to acknowledge her thoughts and opinions as valuable. Your wife is part of the household decision–making team. Over the years, there have been countless times when I have needed Janet's input on a matter. It could have been anything from how to discipline a child to what logo to choose for my business. While I may not always side with her opinion, it still represents an important contribution to the process. I make sure she knows how great her ideas are and how grateful I am to have her for my teammate.

APPRECIATE HER

One of the most therapeutic things to do within a marriage is to rehearse and remember why you fell in love with this person in the first place. Every couple has a love story. Don't ever forget yours. And one of the sexiest things in the world to do is to reminisce and tell your wife what it was that caught your eye and attention. I love to remind Janet that it was her butt in those Jordache jeans that did me in. From the moment she walked by, she had me under her spell. Of course, I go on to tell her how impressed I was with her smile, her kindness, and her heart in general.

Why did you marry her? Of all the girls in the universe, why did this one stand out? Choose not only to recall the reasons, but to continually share them with your wife. This will have healing virtue for the both of you. For your wife, it will let her know that you have not forgotten about your first love. For you, it will be positive reinforcement when so many negative forces are trying to interfere and usurp your attention.

Love goes through a maturation process. When you're not feeling the tingles of yesteryear or your former intense passion, it becomes essential to rehearse your positive history. In the late seventies, Rupert Holmes sang his highest-charting hit, "Escape," later to be known as "The Piña Colada Song." It captures the soul of a man who is disenchanted with his current relationship. He finds himself reading the personal ads, only to become so intrigued by one of the entries that he decides to meet this mystery person at an agreed-upon rendezvous point. The lyrics are as follows:

> *I was tired of my lady, we'd been together too long.*
> *Like a worn-out recording, of a favorite song.*
> *So while she lay there sleeping, I read the*
> *paper in bed.*
>
> *And in the personals column, there was this letter I*
> *read:*

"If you like Piña Coladas, and getting caught in the rain.
If you're not into yoga, if you have half-a-brain.
If you like making love at midnight, in the dunes of the cape.
I'm the lady you've looked for, write to me and escape."

So I waited with high hopes, then she walked in the place.
I knew her smile in an instant, I knew the curve of her face.
It was my own lovely lady, and she said, "Oh, it's you."
Then we laughed for a moment, and I said, "I never knew..."[56]

What he ends up discovering is that his new lover is actually his current lover! These two lovers had more in common than they anticipated and don't need to look any further for what they already have in their relationship. The problem is, we forget about our first love and what attracted us to one another. We start taking our spouse for granted rather than appreciating all her positive qualities.

Value her for who she is. Appreciate her loyalty to your marriage and her commitment to the family.

EDIFY HER

Aaron and Whitney decided to have an honesty session. In their forties now, their sex life was not what they wanted it to be, so they decided to get naked together and tell each other what they didn't like about the other's body. What seemed to be a good idea in theory turned into sexual sabotage, as now Whitney was enlightened to all of her imperfections from Aaron's perspective. Rather than this causing her to want to work out or diet, Whitney now refused to get naked in front of Aaron, again causing a significant strain on their sex life.

Your responsibility as a husband is to love and nurture your wife. You can inspire her to achieve her goals and desires, encourage her in performing her responsibilities, and support her to pursue her dreams. Your uplifting words become a powerful tool and driving force in helping your wife be all that she has the potential to be.

Consider Johnny Lingo. He lived in the South Pacific. The people of Kiniwata Island all spoke very highly of his skills as a tour guide, fisherman, and trader. Yet when it came time for Johnny to find a wife, the islanders still mock his simplemindedness. In their culture, in order to obtain a wife, you paid for her by giving her father cows. Two or three cows would get an average wife, while four to six cows was considered an expensive price and should net a very desirable wife. But Johnny paid an unprecedented eight cows for his wife. The irony is that she was skinny and walked with her shoulders hunched and her head down. She was very shy and backward. The villagers all laughed at Johnny for paying such an extravagant price for such a plain wife and believed his father–in–law must have outwitted him during the dowry negotiations.

Five months after the wedding, a visitor came to the islands to fish and trade and heard the story about Johnny Lingo and his eight–cow wife. When he requested a fishing guide, he was introduced to Johnny. Upon meeting Johnny's wife, the visitor was totally taken back, since she was quite the opposite of everything that had been told him. Paradoxically, she was the most beautiful woman he had ever seen. Her poise and self–confidence radiated an inner beauty. Seeing that the visitor was noticeably surprised, Johnny proceeded to tell of his wife's transformation.

Johnny said, "Before I married her, my wife believed she was worth nothing. As a result, that's the value she projected. I wanted an eight–cow wife. When I paid that for her and treated her in that fashion, she realized that she is worth more than any other woman in the islands and began to behave accordingly. It shows, doesn't it?"[57]

===

"By speaking to your wife in an edifying manner…you have the capacity to raise her to a higher level."

===

By speaking to your wife in an edifying manner, as though she is already everything you want in a woman, you have the capacity to raise her to a higher level. While criticisms and rebukes may sometimes cause a person to try harder, they only serve to reduce a person's self–esteem. Edification can accomplish both—encouraging her while building her up.

SHUT UP AND LISTEN

"A successful marriage requires falling in love many times, always with the same person."

Mignon McLaughlin

For more than fifteen years of my life, I worked as an executive recruiter to a niche market in the insurance industry, placing actuaries within the property and casualty sector. These individuals are well schooled and highly specialized professionals trained to assess the probabilities of financial risk and how it will affect their company's bottom line. Because their knowledge of what they do day in and day out is so far beyond the scope of my training, I have never attempted to go toe–to–toe with them on an intellectual exchange. Rather, I have learned how to ask insightful, strategically timed questions and listen well to their responses, because it is in the listening where the relationship is built and the person knows whether or not I care about them.

Let's suppose that in the course of me trying to recruit someone for a position, one of these actuarial candidates was to tell me that his child is a high school senior and that his family could not consider relocation until the school year finishes out six months from now. On top of that, his wife would have his hide if he even suggested that he was considering a job change before the summer. Nonetheless, I call him the following week with a fantastic out-of-state opportunity that I claim would launch his career. With his ear to the phone, he incredulously listens to my spiel. You can almost see him holding the phone away from his ear and grimacing at it quizzically before he reengages me in conversation and proceeds to ream me out for having the audacity to call him on this. He angrily reminds me of his personal situation. He clearly told me that he couldn't change jobs any time soon, and he especially could not relocate; yet I called him anyway. Instead of looking like the professional I was hoping to portray and winning his confidence, I now appear to be a self-centered, insensitive headhunter who was simply hoping to collect a placement fee at any expense while not caring about the people I represent.

Most people are very inefficient listeners who are able to remember only a small portion of what they hear. Oh, they might have heard you, but were they listening? Have you ever been introduced to someone new? After the initial greeting and requisite name exchange, you may even carry on a cordial conversation with this person. As you walk away, you scratch your head and furrow your brow because you could not remember that person's name if your life depended on it. You definitely heard their name when they first mentioned it, or you would have excused yourself then and there, asking them to repeat it. So it's not that you are a poor hearer. You are a poor listener, failing to focus on something that at the time was simply not that important to you.

The problem with listening is that most people confuse it with hearing. Hearing is a physiological process that results in sending a message to the brain. Listening, on the other hand, requires concentration and making sense of the sounds you hear through this physiological process. There is a clear difference between listening and hearing. To listen is to hear something with thoughtful attention in order to give it your full consideration.

Carry this example into your marriage. Your wife tells you something. It could be anything. "Cheyenne has a dentist appointment next Monday." "Don't forget to buy milk on your way home from work." "Let's make wild, passionate love in the laundry room tonight." Okay, the last one you *would* remember. But the others border on routine and are very easy to dismiss. Besides, our sense of hearing is continually bombarded by information overload through the TV, radio, Internet, cell phones, MP3s, friends, teachers, colleagues, etc. These all carry sounds and information someone wants us to hear and remember.

Listening is an essential part of communication. How does your wife know when you're not listening *or* not *interested* in listening to what she has to say? Well, several things you do can tip her off. Some of the more obvious include nodding off to sleep while she's speaking, yawning, glancing around, shifting in your seat, pacing the floor, responding inappropriately and without understanding, continuing to watch television, clicking away on the computer keyboard, just to name a few. Poor listening results when our minds wander or we tune out too soon. Maybe we're sick, or tired, or plain sick and tired of hearing the same old stuff. Sometimes it's just easier to avoid complex verbal altercations or unsolvable vocal tirades. So rather than focus, we hit the off switch. You can, however, improve your listening skills by becoming more aware of the importance of listening to your wife and the steps you need to take to start becoming better listeners.

Within just a few short years of marriage, Luis had become intolerant of everything about Maria and started openly flirting with other women. His unacceptable behavior ultimately led them to separate. When I met them, Luis had just convinced Maria and the kids to allow him to move back in with them after a long separation. As I confronted him on his past behavior and reasons for the emotional distance in their relationship, Luis sat there silently, looking down at his hands while fumbling with his fingers. He showed no remorse and persistently defended his position by unashamedly blaming Maria for not keeping herself more attractive. Through sobs, Maria pleaded with him to either step up and invest in making their marriage work, or to let her go so that she could move on and make a life for herself and the children independent of him. He just sat there. Needless to point out, this relationship is not headed for recovery unless Luis is willing to learn how to really listen to his wife.

"Listening well is a skill that can be and must be learned."

Most people think that being a good listener is a character trait that comes naturally or that you were born with; therefore, it is rarely taught. In reality, listening well is a skill that can be and must be learned. If you are not predisposed in that direction, it can be quite difficult but not insurmountable. It involves understanding the thoughts and feelings from the speaker's frame of reference—from the "speaker's sneakers," if you will. When you listen to your wife, you should demonstrate interest, concern, and acceptance to what she is saying. Listening is vital to a relationship because it tells your wife she is significant.

- *Be relaxed.* You can always tell when someone has someplace to be or somewhere to go. Make your wife feel like you are exclusively hers for that moment. She has center stage, and you are her devoted audience. Carve out time to talk. If the present is not ideal, or you are fatigued, or the setting is wrong, then set a time and a place to meet.

- *Listen attentively.* Harold likes to talk a lot. And when he does, he expects everyone's complete focus. Ironically, when it is someone else's turn to speak, Harold is looking around as though he is admiring the ceiling paint. Give her your undivided attention. Focused listening lets the speaker know that what they have to say is important to you. When listening, observe your wife for clues about what makes her more comfortable and what makes her less comfortable. And by all means, show interest. Ever have someone yawn in your face as you're speaking to them? It doesn't feel too good. Avoid making distracting motions or gestures. Don't be tossing a ball up in the air and catching it or tapping a drum beat on the table with your fingers. And definitely put the remote control to the television down.

- *Positive body language.* Present yourself in an open way. Crossing your arms appears combative. Slouching on the sofa conveys indifference. Staring into space signals that your mind is elsewhere. Rather, sit or stand comfortably but in a way that says you are engaged and ready to listen. Use positive facial expressions; your countenance speaks volumes. It lets her know how involved you are in what she has to say. Negative facial expressions, like rolling your eyes or grimacing, will close her spirit.

- *Give eye contact.* Wandering glances alert your speaker that you are not entirely committed to this conversation or that you are only willing to listen until a more appealing outside influence comes along. My friend Mark is one of the most gifted listeners I know. We could be in a coliseum filled with thousands of people, but if the two of us are engaged in conversation, you can be sure that his eyes are riveted to my face. It tells me that I'm his sole priority at that moment.

- *Listen actively.* Participate with affirming responses. Give verbal cues to prompt and encourage your wife to say more. These may include little interjections, such as, "Uh-huh," "Really?" "Okay," "Is that so?" "I see," and other conversation-continuing comebacks. These are natural ingredients to promote dialogue, especially if you're truly paying attention. Without these cues, the stark silence becomes disconcerting. Your wife will wonder if she's making sense, if you care, if you're judging her, etc. Of course, don't overdo the talkback, or it will become annoying as well as counterproductive.

- *Don't interrupt.* This includes avoiding the temptation to finish her sentences. Have you ever tried to talk to someone like that? It is probably one of the most annoying habits in the world, although quite easy to do if you've been married for any length of time. Give her a chance to express whatever is on her heart. Sometimes a momentary hesitation or slight delay on your part to respond can force her to search for an even more meaningful word or thought to punctuate her message. Whatever you do, don't break the mood by changing the subject. Human nature likes to deflect negative attention to something else. Remain in the saddle and deal with the issue at hand without interruption.

- *Mirroring.* Repeat back to her in your own words what you think you heard her say. How many times has the listener heard and acted upon something different than what the speaker was trying to convey? This does not mean you agree with her but rather understand what she is saying. Ask her if you got it. I do this whenever I go through the drive–thru window of a fast–food restaurant. After placing my order, I always ask the person on the other end to repeat my order. This way we are both on the same page, and there are no surprise outcomes when I pick up my meal—and my burger doesn't have mustard on it!

- *Don't be anxious to take back the lead.* For most of us, our favorite subject to talk about is "me." If confronted we may want to explain our behavior or justify our actions. To that end we are waiting for our opportunity to jump in and control the tempo. Or we may try and "one–up" the speaker with a better example of our own. No one wants to hear a story about someone else who is irrelevant to the conversation at hand. Denise was notorious for this. Any time you told her something, in her innocent, yet desperate desire to relate, she always had a better story. While well meaning, it killed the moment.

- *Don't try and fix everything for her.* One of the most common tendencies of a man is to come to his wife's rescue. This chivalry has been recorded ever since the knight in shining armor responded to the cries of the helpless maiden. Let your woman unload without reprisals or repercussions or recommendations. Don't correct or give advice. Sometimes she just wants to be heard, so let her vent. After all, she's not looking for you to be her father or therapist, just a friend for the moment.

- *Show empathy.* Be compassionate. Show that you care. Say "I'm sorry" if the conversation warrants it. Perhaps she just needs you to hold her hand or give her a hug to let her know it will be all right.

- *Remain open–minded and objective.* If you are too emotionally absorbed, you will tend to hear what you want to hear, not what is actually being said. Put your own agenda and defenses aside and learn to really listen.

Being a good listener requires effort, patience, concentration, and a sincere interest in or willingness to listen to her knowledge, ideas, and viewpoints. Listening to your wife encourages and confirms her value as a communicator and a person who has valuable knowledge to share.

Listening will most definitely improve the results you achieve in your marriage relationship. When people don't listen well, either because of conflicting viewpoints or lack of skill, the exchange is slow, time is wasted, and motivation is sapped. The effect is like flying into a headwind and getting a lot of resistance from making progress. When couples do listen well, misunderstandings get cleared up, marriages are energized, and time is saved. The effect of listening well is like having the wind at your back and making significant headway toward your goals. Blake tries to talk things out with Hannah but only gets resistance from her. When they came to counsel with us, Hannah opened up like a parakeet whistling to lure its mate. Blake was flabbergasted by her openness and inquired why Hannah wouldn't talk that freely to him at home. What he discovered is that Hannah did not feel safe to say the things she said without mediators in her corner. Blake tends to hear only what he wants to hear and not give credence to her feelings. So in her mind, why bother exposing her vulnerability?

As melodramatic as this might sound, consider yourself forewarned: If you do not listen well, you will never be successful in your marriage. Miscommunications will take place. Misunderstandings will occur. Misstatements will increase—all because you do not understand what your wife is trying to say. To that end, I strive to learn how to hear not only what she is saying, but also what she means. Men are usually very literal in what they hear and how they translate. When your wife says, "We never spend any time together," she is not looking for you to refute her by taking out your planner and showing her that three weeks ago this past Thursday you met her for coffee while waiting for your car to be repaired. What she is trying to say is that she misses you and desperately needs to make an intimate connection with you. Or if she should say, "The only way things get done around here is if I do them myself," this is simply a plea for appreciation and assistance, not an opportunity for you to brag about washing the dishes last Monday. Be sensitive to her language and try not to be defensive.

Remember that listening is the process of understanding or decoding the speaker's message. Not only do you hear it, but you register it as well. While it may seem like a pretty straightforward process, it remains as one of the key offenses wives have against their husbands. Take time to develop this simple skill and take your relationship to the next level.

KILL HER WITH KINDNESS

> "Only two things are necessary to keep one's wife happy. One is to let her think she is having her own way, the other, to let her have it."
> Lyndon B. Johnson

Wouldn't it be great if we could all just be nice to one another? It sounds so simplistic that I'm almost embarrassed to write it out. Consider the wonderful, warm holiday spirit that seems to captivate hearts everywhere during the Christmas season, and try to capture it as though it were some mystical essence you could market to consumers. As you observe people busily scurrying about during this special time of year, you hear countless stories of kindness and giving that can practically melt your heart. O. Henry depicted this Christmas sentiment in his uplifting short story *The Gift of the Magi.* For in it you witness the greatest sacrifice of love as Della cuts her prized hair to buy Jim a chain for his pocket watch. While she was busy consummating her sacrificial act of love unbeknownst to him, Jim went and sold that very same heirloom pocket watch in order to buy Della a set of expensive combs to adorn her long, flowing hair that she had just cut.[58] The ultimate irony…Mark Twain put it this way, "Kindness is a language which the deaf can hear and the blind can read."[59] Kindness is recognizable by all.

We all like to be the recipient of someone else's kindness. Let's first learn to give out kindness so that others may benefit from it.

YOUR WIFE IS YOUR GIFT

It seems like yesterday when our daughter Rachelle was sixteen years old and interested in dating a young man from school. The rule in our house was that the male suitor must request an audience with me in order to ask permission to spend time with my daughter. My psychology behind this was severalfold: a) I wanted to make sure the young man knew I was very involved in my daughter's life. This would keep him accountable to me; b) the young man had to be mature enough to have a conversation with his love interest's "old man." If he could not step it up to have an adult conversation with me, then he obviously was not ready to spend time with my daughter; and c) our meeting would give me a chance to find out his intentions while communicating my expectations regarding their relationship. More succinctly put, it would give me the opportunity to put the fear of God (and Dad) in him.

As a matter of fact, I even told Rachelle that when the young man showed up at my door, it was my intention to plant the biggest, fattest, juiciest kiss on his lips and tell him, "Just remember…whatever you do to my daughter, I *will* do to you." Rachelle half smiled and laughed nervously, not entirely sure if I were kidding.

I came to find out that it took this high school–aged young man a full six months to gather enough bravado to call me to set up our meeting. Yes, he had to call me directly; I would not let Rachelle intervene on his behalf. When he finally mustered up the courage, I politely invited him over, ready for our long–awaited interrogation session. Although I had several questions that I posed to get more acquainted with this young man, what I really wanted to convey to him was the incredible worth of my daughter.

When he arrived, I met him in the driveway and escorted him to our outside patio in the backyard. We sat across from one another at a table on our back deck, while my wife and daughter anxiously peered through the slats of the blinds hanging from the living room windows. After an obligatory exchange of introductory civilities, I ended up telling him in story form:

"A king possessed a rare, expensive diamond uncovered in a remote African mine, and it was given to him as a special keepsake. It was a one–of–a–kind gemstone that was irre-

placeable and irreproducible. The king treasured that dia-
mond, frequently holding it and polishing it for prominent
display in his showcase. One day a visiting dignitary came for
a visit. After securing the king's trust, the king unlocked his
display case and showed his guest his most prized possession.
The guest looked upon it with awe, not even daring to touch
the diamond for fear of leaving fingerprints or risking drop-
ping or damaging such a great treasure. This show–and–tell
continued for each of that guest's successive visits with the
king.

"With little forewarning the king was called out of town.
He needed a caretaker for his treasure—someone he could
completely trust. Someone who would not only clean and
polish the diamond, but would also guard it with his life,
recognizing its extraordinary worth. The king decided to call
upon his special guest, who by now had become a trusted
friend. With what sense of responsibility do you think the
guest would attend to this matter? Would he dare jeopardize
his trust with the king by losing or damaging the diamond?
Or allowing it to be stolen? On the contrary! This friend did
all he could to care for the king's priceless treasure. He knew
of its amazing value and wanted to give it back in even bet-
ter condition than he found it. That way he could please the
king."

I then proceeded to tell the young suitor that my
daughter is that rare diamond. She is one of a kind, irreplaceable, and irreproducible. I expect her to be treated
with the utmost respect, handling her as one would a

delicate treasure. If I should ever entrust her to his care, then I will expect that she is safeguarded and returned to my home in as good—no, even better—condition than when I first handed her over to him. As a dad, I knew the incredible worth of my daughter and expected a man to treat her with dignity and high regard. Corny as it may seem, he completely got the picture.

King Solomon, known for his incomparable wisdom, declared that the man who gets a wife receives a good gift.[60] Your spouse is one of the greatest gifts you could ever have been given. You have been entrusted to forge a lifelong union with another human being. With that comes tremendous responsibility. Cheer your bride on. Help her become all she can be. Encourage her. Affirm her. Love her. In so doing, the same will be returned to you.

GIVE KINDNESS EVEN WHEN SHE DOES NOT DESERVE IT

Consider the following letter written by a man to his friends boasting about his kindness toward his wife in spite of her shortcomings:

Men must remember that as women grow older it's harder for them to maintain the same quality of housekeeping. When men notice this, they should try not to yell. Let me relate how I handle the situation. When I took early retirement, it became necessary for Nancy to get a full–time job. Shortly after she started working I noticed she was beginning to show her age. I usually get home from fishing about the same time she gets home from work. Although she knows how hungry I am after fishing all day, she almost always has to take some time to unwind a bit before she starts supper. I try not to yell, instead I tell her to take her time and just wake me up when she does get supper on the table. She used to do the dishes as soon as we finished eating. Now they sit several hours after supper. I do what I can by reminding her each evening that they aren't cleaning themselves. I know she appreciates this, as it does seem to motivate her to get them done before she goes to bed. The good news is that waiting to clean the dishes also gives her more time to do things like shampoo the dog, dust the furniture, and vacuum the carpet. And if I've had a good day fishing, it gives her the opportunity to gut and scale the fish at a more leisurely pace. Now I know that I probably look like a saint in the way I support Nancy. However, guys, if you just yell at your wife a little less often because of this letter, writing it was worthwhile.

Signed,

Bob

P.S. Bob's funeral was on Saturday.

P.P.S. Nancy was acquitted on Monday.[61]

Though comical, some guys just don't get it. Being married to someone for a lifetime can seem quite daunting. Think about it. Someone will get to see and know everything about you. She gets to see you at your best, and she gets to see you at your worst. She gets to see you dressed to the nines, and she gets to see you in your bedroom clothes when you wake up in the morning. Similarly, you get to witness her highs and lows as well. Unless you are perfect, you are bound to mess up a time or two at some point during your lifetime. And your spouse will be there to witness it and vice versa.

Don't require a performance–based marriage. Your wife should not have to earn your kindness. So often we are guilty of playing mind games with ourselves. *Why should I be kind when she's not kind to me? I'm always the one who has to initiate.* Which brings up a great question: Whose responsibility is it to be kind first? Who should make the first move? As men, let's not make this a difficult standoff. Instead, take the initiative and choose to practice kindness.

DO FOR HER WHAT YOU WOULD LIKE DONE FOR YOU

When we consider the Golden Rule for living, we need to keep in mind our gender differences. She may not appreciate everything you might if the roles were reversed. In other words, you have to think in terms of her world. Just because you want a passionate romp in the sack right at this very moment, don't assume that is her desire. She may be more grateful if the house was tidied up a bit and the kids were fed and taken care of.

Try this self–test: Do you spend more time thinking about what you can do for her or what was the last thing she did for you? If you're keeping score, then married life will be very long as well as disappointing. But if you're all about blessing her, then each day presents fresh opportunities. Just realize that you're not doing someone a favor if they don't appreciate it. I once tried to buy Janet a blender for her birthday. After she threatened to put my cheeseburger in it and serve it for dinner, I got the hint. I won't make that mistake again.

Sal is a type–A obsessive–compulsive personality. Not only does he like to perfectly organize his own belongings, but he can't stand it if Patti's stuff is out of order. Without notice or permission, he will empty out her dresser drawers and closet in order to fold and color code everything. Some women may think, *I wish my husband would do that for me,* but Patti feels violated. She completely recognizes Sal's narcissistic efforts to satisfy his own dysfunctional need for order without regard for her feelings. Kindness must always be doled out with the other person's best interests in mind, not your own agenda.

Janet likes it when I buy her a little gift outside of celebrating a special occasion. But if I were to buy her something that she did not appreciate—a history book or a variety pack of beef jerky—then even though I may have committed a kind act, its value is lost because of the recipient's aversion toward those items. Like so many men, I can play the martyr and visit a shrink in order to tell him how unappreciated I am and that every time I try to show my wife kindness she only rejects it. On the surface I may even seem like the victim. The truth is that I am not considering her at all, only satiating my need to look good.

Isn't this the way many of us live out our marriages? We say or do things at home that we think should be recognized and applauded, but honestly, if we had taken the time to learn our spouse's interests or filtered it through past experiences with her, then we would be more aware of what she actually appreciates. When you do for her what you would like done for you, take into account the bigger picture.

DON'T COMPARE YOUR RELATIONSHIP TO OTHERS

Kurt was one of those guys, nice as can be, but liked to micromanage his household. If Alicia wanted to repaint a room in the house, she would have to clear the color scheme with him. He required her to inform him before rearranging any of their furniture or decorations. Whenever she wanted a new outfit to wear or a knick-knack for the house, she had to ask his permission. As you might imagine, anytime we went for a visit to Kurt and Alicia's house, I always left feeling much better about myself and my marriage. It's not that our relationship was so stellar; I was just happy it was a lot better than Kurt's.

Just because you're doing better than the couple next to you doesn't mean you have a great relationship. And just because you're treating your girl better than most of the other guys you know—that still doesn't mean that you are loving her your best. I am guilty of this one. I think I'm pretty helpful around the house. I often make the bed, clean up the dishes, run to the supermarket to pick up groceries, and travel with my wife whenever she has to run errands that really don't involve me. So because I do a lot of those routine, pesky tasks, the tendency is to think I'm a pretty decent guy—especially compared to most of the husbands I know. Because of that it is easy for me to become complacent from taking my kindness to the next level since I think she should appreciate what I already do. The reality is that I often ignore the "extras" that I'm aware I could focus on.

Any seasoned husband should know quite well what is important to his wife. If within your circle of friends you happen to stand out as the man who is really nice to his wife, then congratulations. Not only keep up the good work, but try to take it up a notch. On the other hand, if you see a guy treating his wife better than you do yours, then it's time to step up and begin to treat her with the kindness you promised her and that she expected when you first married her.

BE CONSIDERATE IN THE SMALL THINGS

Showing kindness to your wife can take on many forms. It doesn't always have to be a Disneyland experience. Handle the everyday matters by remembering the little, practical things. Attention to detail carries a lot of weight when it comes to expressing your love for someone.

In way of an example, let me relate it to my son. I remember when Chandler had his mind made up on what he wanted for Christmas. Being a seven–year–old boy, he had his heart set on a particular kind of army tank or aircraft carrier. G.I. Joe had released a series of these vehicles that were quickly bought up, but we remained determined to track them down. We went from Toys 'R Us to Wal–Mart to Target to Kay–Bee Toys trying to find just the right assemblage of pieces. Eventually accomplishing our task, we wrapped the pieces carefully and hid them inconspicuously under the back of our Christmas tree. When that special day finally arrived and it came time to open presents, Chandler was not disappointed, nor were we as he squealed his excitement over each of the gifts and gave us several running–bear hug tackles to show his gratitude. He couldn't believe that we remembered the details of his wish list. It is critical to note that we did not have to elaborate on the great lengths we undertook to make it happen for him.

That's what love does. It goes out of its way to make things better for someone else without requiring special recognition. So focus on blessing your wife by doing those sacrificial little things to let her know that you're thinking of her.

Growing up on Long Island, my dad was a New York City policeman. Each month, he would have his weekly turn at the graveyard shift that ended in the early morning hours. Due to his lengthy commute, he usually got home while I was still asleep in bed. He would quietly prepare for his off–hour nap trying not to wake anyone. With Dad finally tucked away sleeping, I would then have to leave for school. Dad did something really special during that time. In order to let me know that he was thinking of me, he frequently brought me a goody bag that might have included some assortment of comic books, gum, candy, and baseball cards. Even though we did not see each other on those mornings, it was from this simple gesture that I knew my dad had me on his mind.

Let your wife know that she is on your mind. What can you do to let your partner know that you are thinking about her? Don't keep her wondering.

"Any guy can sweep any girl off her feet; he just needs the right broom."

Will Smith, from the movie *Hitch*

SOMETIMES KINDNESS IS BEST CONVEYED NOT BY OUR ACTIONS, BUT THROUGH OUR REACTIONS

As our family drove up to our house, we immediately noticed water streaming down the driveway. *Hmm,* I thought. *That's strange. It's not even raining.* It was unmistakably apparent that the water source was emanating from the side–entrance door next to the garage that led into the laundry room. All of a sudden, Janet's memory alarm was triggered. She had run the water in the wash-basin to rinse out the mop before we left home and never turned off the faucet—probably distracted by the kids. The sink had filled to capacity and had been overflowing for the past three hours.

Apprehensively, we entered the laundry room, not fully knowing what to expect. There in a cage, struggling to keep her head above water level, completely soaked and straining for breath was our newly acquired Shih–Tzu puppy, Paris. What a pathetic sight. She was yelping for aid while instinctively doing the dog paddle. We quickly rescued her from her unlikely prison and wrapped a large bath towel around her while we held her tightly for comfort. She was shivering from her traumatic near–death experience.

Water had escaped into the central area of our home, saturated the hardwood floors, and poured down into our terrace level. Since Janet is an interior designer, let me elaborate on our finished terrace level. It meant that everything was completely furnished and accessorized and maxed out, looking nicer than most people's main living areas.

Overwhelmed, we quickly made a visual assessment of the damages. We would have to repair and repaint walls, refinish hardwood floors, replace carpets and padding, change out ceiling tiles, and take inventory of all the damaged stuff—from accessories to electronics—as the water knew no boundaries on this subterranean level.

Our homeowner's insurance agent directed us to a flood–repair company. They responded quickly and commenced the clean–up process resulting from the water damage. Their people worked through the night to absorb and sop up the excess water while systematically placing large fans throughout the rooms to accelerate the drying process.

As I observed the overall damage, I was speechless. I couldn't yell. I couldn't cry. I couldn't console or reassure my wife that it would be okay. I was numb. In her nervousness, Janet is prone to laughing, which made the situation more stressful for me. She desperately wanted me to say something—anything—but it was one of those rare wordless moments for me.

Then, as if I had my own epiphany, I was reminded of another recent event. Just days earlier I was refilling our backyard hot tub and forgot to turn off the water spigot. I left the house to conduct some business and completely forgot about it. Returning home, I went into my home office and resumed business as usual. When I finally remembered that I had previously been filling the hot tub, I had that terrorized realization. Rushing out to the backyard, I saw what I already knew to be so—that the hot tub had been overflowing for hours. What a dreadful waste of water. Thankfully, besides the extra utility expense, the worst outcome was that the surrounding plants and flowerbeds drank a whole lot more than they needed.

My mind came back to the current situation, and I knew that Janet's simple mistake could have happened to any one of us—including me. When she flooded our laundry room, powder room, main hallway, and basement, I could have sanctimoniously chastised her, belittling her forgetfulness. Instead, I was confronted with my own humanity and able to give grace and support instead. Accidents happen; let's make an effort to be tender toward our spouses when they already feel vulnerable in these moments. Overreacting, scolding, and criticizing never help an already-stressful situation. I was able to rally around her, reassure her, and deal with the matter in such a way that she knew I was not holding her to blame.

Kindness is more than words; it is even more than deeds. It is often found in your reactions and responses.

HAVE A MARRIAGE OF NO REGRETS

Why is it so often easier to be kind to people who are outside our family? Probably because we know that our wives are not going anywhere and there are usually no visible immediate repercussions. That's why it is so easy to take our mates for granted and cause them to feel taken advantage of. In actuality, the best place to start kindness should be in our own home.

Ronald Reagan said, "There is no greater happiness for a man than approaching a door at the end of a day knowing someone on the other side of that door is waiting for the sound of his footsteps."[62] As a husband, doesn't that sound like the ultimate fulfillment—to know that your wife is anxious and eager to be with you? The only way to achieve that level of satisfaction in your relationship is to love her with abandonment.

Do the right thing because it's the right thing to do, not because you are expecting accolades and curtain calls. Most of the kindness you show behind closed doors will never be known by the multitudes—just by your wife. You are only responsible for your own actions, not for her actions or responses toward yours. If you can adopt that mind-set, you will be well on your way to actively seizing some control toward the success of your marriage.

HE'S TOUCHING ME ...

"It is not a lack of love, but a lack of friendship that makes unhappy marriages."

Friedrich Nietzsche

What makes a man irresistible to a woman is not how *interesting* he is, but how *interested* he is in her. A man must actively practice pursuing his wife, and that pursuit begins with showing her affection. Since affection is one of the chief needs of a woman, make sure you give your wife plenty of it without reservation or conservation. While some men may grow up in a house where they experienced a healthy dose of affection, others may not have. Many men only discover how to become affectionate from their wives after they are already married. Others may have learned a thing or two from relationships they had prior to their current marriage. Unfortunately, some men have simply never learned a sincere, selfless way to show affection. The good news is, affection can be taught and learned. There is always today to begin!

> "What makes a man irresistible to a
> woman is not how *interesting* he is,
> but how *interested* he is in her."

AFFECTION: PHYSICAL TOUCH

Affection is kindness, compassion, love, sympathy, tenderness, patience, understanding, gentleness, thoughtfulness, generosity—all wrapped up into an outward expression. When we think of affection, we promptly think about hugs, kisses, holding hands, and many other physical displays. While these are all part of it, affection can also be demonstrated through verbal or non–physical means. You can show affection through compliments, endearing terms, affirming messages, and many other spoken words. Non–touch affections are critically essential to the health of your relationship, which is why we have already spent an entire chapter discussing it, *Compliment Her... or Someone Else Will.*

Physical touch is a marital privilege. It should be nurtured but never taken for granted. Touch your wife as often as you think about it and whenever the chemistry between the two of you allows. I like to watch people at the beach as they prepare to make their way into the ocean water. Some run in with abandonment and dive headfirst at the earliest sign that the water is deep enough to swallow their body. Others gingerly place their foot in the water and quickly pull it out because of the cold, practically shocking temperature. Then they take their time getting acclimated to the cold sensation by gradually easing their way in, one body section at a time. Many of us may use the same strategies with physical touch. When you are advancing in the physical form of affection with your mate, timing is everything. There are times to throw caution to the wind, and there are times to test the waters. Also, it is of utmost importance to learn what kind of touches she likes and dislikes.

Mitch and Doreen were sitting around the table playing "The Newlywed Game"[63] with some of their couple friends. A question arose that went something like, "What will your husband say he does that drives you nuts?" Of course, the husband is supposed to guess his wife's response in order to answer the question correctly and win points. The irony was that when Doreen responded, Mitch was not only surprised but devastated when he learned that nibbling on his wife's ear was a complete turnoff to her—especially since he had been doing that for the past ten years and all along sweet Doreen was torturously enduring his attempt at sexual foreplay.

All that to say, make an effort to understand her preferences. Try some of these out for size:

- Scratch her head and mess her hair (as long as she is already in for the night).

- Caress her face, outlining all her contours and features.

- Brush her hair.

- Gently rub up and down her forearm as you are sitting next to her.

- Tickle her palm and massage her fingers.

- Kiss her neck in a way that tells her you think she is sexy.

- Peck her on the cheek.

- Don't just kiss her lips; taste her lips.

- Softly nibble on her earlobe as you whisper a secret.

- Bear hug her as though you can't get enough of her.

- Lay her head across your lap as you stroke her face.

- Give her a footbath and then put lotion on her feet.

- Massage her shoulders using body oils.

- Scratch her back (for more than five seconds).

- Inhale her scent like you have never smelled anything so enchanting.

- Hold her hand when you walk.

- Put your arm around her and cuddle.

- Spoon with her as you lie together.

- Pat her on the bottom (as long as the setting is appropriate).

- Sensually wash her body as you shower together.

Men need to understand how strongly women need these affectionate affirmations. From a woman's point of view, affection is the quintessential ingredient of her relationship.

An older couple was lying in bed one night. The husband was falling asleep, but the wife was in a romantic mood and wanted to talk. She said, "You used to hold my hand when we were courting."

Wearily he reached across, held her hand for a second, and tried to get back to sleep.

A few moments later she said, "Then you used to kiss me."

Mildly irritated, he reached across, gave her a peck on the cheek, and settled down to sleep.

Recognizing their progress, thirty seconds later she said, "Then you used to bite my neck."

Angrily, he threw back the bed covers and got out of bed.

"Where are you going?" she asked incredulously.

"To get my teeth!"[64]

To most women, offering our affection through physical touch symbolizes our love, protection, honor, concern, and approval toward them. When a husband shows his wife affection, he is sending a message:

- A well–timed kiss boasts, "I love you and I'm glad you're mine."

- A strong hug suggests, "I'll take care of you and protect you."

- Holding her face close to yours and looking into her eyes says, "You are important to me."

- Placing a strong, reassuring hand on her shoulder implies, "I'm here for you. We're in this together."

- A high–five or congratulatory squeeze affirms, "Great job! I'm so proud of you."

As her husband, you have the privilege of navigating and learning the landscape of her body. Find her tickle spots. Learn her erogenous zones. Stay away from her "that–makes–me–want–to–punch–you" areas. (Ask me how I know this…)

"There is a place you can touch a woman that will drive her crazy. Her heart."

Melanie Griffith, from the movie *Milk Money*

Men need to learn the art of sexless affection—touching, holding, rubbing, squeezing, massaging, tickling, scratching, caressing, hugging—without ulterior motives. Don't just give affection as your prerequisite foreplay to lovemaking. Your touch should make her feel wanted, needed, secure, and protected—never violated. And oh, it bears repeating, timing is everything here. There may be times when she does not want to be touched. She may even want to be left alone. It's her body, and you need to respect that. Don't take it personally and get your feelings hurt if she rejects your advances. Be understanding and get ready to try again when the timing and setting are more conducive.

ROMANCE: KEEPING IT ALIVE

Romance is one of those abstract properties that can mean different things to different people. Although being romantic may not be exactly definable, it is certainly describable. Just ask any woman, as they seem to have an innate grasp on the concept since, for her, it is what she most desires out of a relationship. At a minimum, we understand that any act of romance involves doing something to express one's love or affection in a uniquely meaningful way. Loving someone is easy; converting that affection into romance is the difficult part. While you can find countless romantic ideas on the Internet, in movies and books, true romance is a personalized expression packaged in sincerity and originality.

I asked my wife to enlighten me on what makes the difference between a kind act I might render that lets her know how much I love her and something she would gauge as being romantic. How can I turn doing something sweet for her, like buying her a candle or taking her out to lunch, into something that she considers romantic? From what I am able to comprehend, it's all in the presentation.

Let's dissect it a bit further…It's one thing to buy a candle; it's another to wait until the children are in bed or away from the house and then to light the candle and turn on some music in order to set a private atmosphere with a soothing mood. Although taking her out for lunch may be a very thoughtful and generous gesture, it may have a sense of ordinary to it. A romantic lunch would require a bit more preparation or creativity. That's why women like it when we pack a picnic basket or make special reservations at an out–of–the–way restaurant and then have chilled champagne or flowers waiting at the table. Our partners want to know they are important enough for us to go the extra mile by exercising some planning and forethought.

Continuing our analysis, you can purchase concert tickets for her favorite musical group and that would be a very special gift. But for it to be romantic, you must add an impractical and somewhat personalized twist to it. Maybe get chauffeured there in a limousine or arrange a way to surprise her with the tickets. Going to the beach with the family is fantastic. But for it to be romantic, make sure the kids are taken care of and then go for a barefoot walk along the shoreline in the moonlight while you're holding her hand. Picking out a girly movie and watching it at home together is very selfless and thoughtful, but it's not enough. In order for it to be romantic, try preparing for her some unique appetizers (not Bagel Bites and frozen pizza). Make sure the fireplace is crackling, and arrange place settings using elegant dishware on a fluffy comforter so the two of you can eat and cuddle on the floor while watching the movie. Make sure you assume charge for serving her as well as cleaning up the mess. Are you getting the picture?

Regardless of what the cynics may say, chivalry is still in. Whether it comes from a suave Casanova or a rugged Indiana Jones, women appreciate being treated with old–fashioned respect and manners. There was something special about the days when a gentleman would drape his coat over a puddle so that she wouldn't get her feet wet or surrender his umbrella to her to shield her from the rain. Learn how to be romantic without having sexual expectations in return. There are a few other measures you can take to add romance to your relationship.

> "Learn how to be romantic without having sexual expectations in return."

Personalize It

You can't approach romance with a one–size–fits–all strategy, expecting the usual teddy bears, jewelry, chocolates, and flowers to be the all–encompassing answer for every occasion. Recognize that romantic settings are usually private—just for the two of you. It should also be personalized—that is, knowing her well enough so that you can do something for her that she would actually appreciate. Just because you go out of your way to take her ballroom dancing or make an appointment for her with a renowned tattoo artist, that doesn't mean that she would necessarily find that romantic unless those are things that are specifically meaningful to her. You ought to take initiative to find out her hobbies, interests, secrets, and fantasies so that you can personalize whatever romantic strides you attempt. When your inspired efforts are solely motivated for her pleasure, you have a winning formula for romance.

There are certain acts that are romantic no matter how you slice it. If I hire an airplane to skywrite "I love you, Janet" while the two of us are relaxing on the beach at sunset, we would all agree that's pretty romantic for anyone. But here's the irony…What may be romantic for one couple is not always romantic for another. Keep in mind, romance must reflect a personalized special effort. If a husband never helps out around the house and one day shockingly decides to let his wife rest on the couch while he does the cleaning and attends to her needs, she would consider that pretty romantic. Whereas another woman who is already accustomed to her husband's domestic support would think that is very kind but not necessarily romantic. Different strokes for different folks.

Return to Your First Love

I've heard that married men can rightly be compared to hunters. They hunt, kill, bag their game, and head on home. Unfortunately, in this example the wife is often the "game." Once conquered, the man subconsciously perceives that he no longer has the challenge of conquest, so rather than diligently romancing her, he begins to take her for granted. After a steady diet of feeling undervalued and unappreciated, the woman forfeits her sense of significance in the marriage and turns an emotional corner. Don't wait until you're about to lose her before you begin to introduce romantic innovation back into your relationship.

Treat her the way you did when you first met before the two of you actually became an item. How did you act to show her you were interested? When you wanted to impress her, what would you do? Behave like you did back then in order to win her over—like you're competing for her attention.

Date your mate. One day the children will be gone, and what will you have left? Have you invested enough interest in your wife for the two of you to now enjoy the next season of your life together? Being self–employed carries a lot of demands, but one initiative I enacted was to finish my workweek by noon every Friday. At that point, I would not take any more business phone calls or messages. Janet and I would then venture out for a private lunch date adhering to an agreed–upon two–part rule: 1) No fast food, and 2) it had to be a place we had not eaten before. That season of our life was very enjoyable because we invested time in one another and got to appreciate many new dining experiences.

It's not rocket science to implement a few novel measures that can keep your love fresh and new. However, it does take a decision to want to and a commitment to follow through, and that's where so many of us fail. People will do what's most important to them. The health of your relationship will reflect your investment in it.

Be Creative

On a chilly winter evening, a husband and wife were snuggled together on the floor watching television. With the kids already asleep, they finally had some much–coveted alone time. During a commercial break, he reached over and gave her foot a gentle squeeze.

"Mmmm," she said expectantly. "That's sweet."

"Actually," he admitted, "I thought that was the remote."[65]

Life can be full of monotony and routine. Don't let your marriage become its latest victim. It's very easy to fall into the trap of predictability and repetition. We all recognize that routine is a necessary part of marriage and family life. You must get up and go to work every day, get the kids ready for school, eat your meals, attend to recurring responsibilities, and the like. But don't let this regimen become the noose that stifles your imagination and inventiveness when it comes to your marriage relationship.

Learn how to set the mood. In addition to timing, lighting and sound play a critical role for setting a romantic atmosphere. There is something alluring about dim lighting, whether sunrise, sunset, moonlight, lowlights, or candlelight. Music also plays a key part in contributing to the perfect ambiance. Do you find intimate dinner conversation more enjoyable listening to hip–hop music blaring louder than your voices or if elevator music was playing softly in the background?

Case in point…I could barge into our kitchen while my wife is feeding lunch to the children and give her a spectacular four–carat tennis bracelet for no occasion. I would have done an extraordinary feat that any woman would be envious of. My wife would be very excited and appreciative, but my action would not necessarily be classified as romantic. If, on the other hand, I crept in while the house was quiet and closed the curtains, shutting out the invading sunshine, lit a few candles, turned on some faint symphonic background music, and then invited my wife into the room. Rather than impatiently thrusting the jewelry upon her, I begin to tell her how much she means to me and that I know I don't deserve her. At that point, I take out a meticulously gift–wrapped box with a neat red bow on top (red being her favorite color). With that I say, "This is just a little something to let you know how much I love you." Which scenario do you think has the greater impact on her? And which is more romantic?

Men are more creative, imaginative, and romantic than they give themselves credit for if they could just be willing to make the effort. When you first started dating the love of your life, both of you were on your best behavior. Everything was so exciting and stimulating because it was all so new. That was the excitement of the unknown. Husbands want to know why she doesn't emotionally respond as she did when you first got married. Maybe it's because you're not treating her the way you did when you first married. Don't let the honeymoon be the romantic pinnacle of your relationship together. It doesn't have to go downhill from there.

In order for romance to thrive, be willing to reintroduce the exhilaration that characterized the beginning of your relationship. Be spontaneous and creative. Attempt to do things out of the ordinary to keep your partner guessing.

It's the Little Things that Count

Lest I mislead you to believe that romance must always be an over–the–top display of ingenuity and surprise, it can also be found in the little things you do for her on a daily basis. In fact, sometimes the most romantic moments are simple, spontaneous, and free. Find unique ways to tell her how much you love her. Over the years, I've done what I can to keep things fresh for Janet by leaving her notes on her pillow, in her lunch bag or suitcase, attached to something in the refrigerator, on her computer screen, or under the windshield wipers. I've driven to where I know she parked the car just to leave a folded note on the side–view mirror or to write "I love you" with my finger on her driver–side window. My motivation is imagining how I might bring a smile to her face.

Start thinking about how you might bless her with no strings attached. Put on a fancy suit and tie to take her out for ice cream. Draw her bubble bath and leave rose petals floating on the water's surface. Exercise gentility by opening her car door, pulling out her seat when she sits, warming up her vehicle on cold mornings, or starting the car and running the air conditioner for her on particularly hot days. Write out a greeting card for no occasion and leave it somewhere she'll find it when you are not even around.

Be thankful for your wife and don't take her for granted. When you're around someone all the time and get to see each other's faults, it's so easy to overlook how amazing she is. Remember why you married her in the first place and treat her with the same tribute you did when you first met.

If you implement efforts to be romantic and your wife just doesn't seem to respond with appreciation or acknowledgment, don't despair or take it as rejection. Perhaps you've caught her off guard or she's going through a stressful situation. Truthfully, she may be wondering what you want from her since you've never acted this way before. Let her see a lifestyle change in you so you can build trust with her. And, as always, find a way to talk it through with her.

SEX: ANYWHERE, ANYTIME

He said, "Ever since I first laid eyes on you, I've wanted to make love to you in the worst way."

"Well," she said, "you've succeeded."[66]

One of the biggest challenges within marriage is shared sexual gratification. It might be the understatement of the year, but men and women typically have different sex drives. Facing this opposing reality, how can you reach a mutually satisfying relationship? Many married people complain that earlier in their marriage there was much more sexual pleasure and fulfillment. Teasing, playfulness, exploration, and experimentation were all part of the great seduction. Provocative glances and suggestive whispers told it all. Romance was at its peak. Whether doing it in the laundry room or the closet or on top of your Harley, you couldn't get enough of each other. And then after a while, the embers of passion seem to slowly fade to a steady glow or, for some, die out altogether.

We need to understand that love goes through a progressive maturation process. In the beginning of our marriage, lovemaking is brand new and ready to be tested out to its fullest. But, like anything, the newness eventually wears off, and we begin to treat each other more commonplace while holding on to our gender–driven expectations of sex. It's not that we love each other less. But if we use the frequency of our lovemaking as the test, it might seem so. See if you can relate to the following story.

Stella had just finished a long day of tedious, hands–on work. She was on her feet all day. It seemed like anything that could go wrong went wrong during her shift. Because she was the senior person on that line, the supervisor came down hard on her for lagging behind their daily production quota. Emotionally spent and with the workday finally behind her, she bolted from the shop to pick up the kids from after–school care. Half listening to their jibber jabber concerning their day, Stella was more focused on all the evening's responsibilities still in front of her, including what she would be preparing for dinner before Frank got home. With kids in tow, she stopped at the grocery store to pick up a few essentials and went through the drive–thru at the dry cleaners to collect Frank's dress shirts. Now the real race began: change out of her work clothes, tidy up around the house, begin dinner preparations, set the table, and start kids on their homework. At least, thankfully, the boys did not have ball practice tonight.

When Frank arrived, he was his usual self. He gave Stella an obligatory greeting with an unemotional peck on the cheek as though she were his aunt Sophia stopping by for a visit. He kicked his shoes off, said a quick hello to the children, and plopped down in his recliner to read the newspaper.

"When's dinner?" he inquired, his predictability almost like clockwork.

The family sat down and ate together, engaging in the routine roundtable conversational exchange.

"How was your day?"

"Good."

"How about yours?"

"Good."

"What's new?"

"Nothing."

After dinner, Frank retired from the table, leaving the cleanup to his wife and children. In his mind he had worked hard today and deserved some time to wind down. Stella spearheaded the kitchen duties, saw to it that the kids' homework got completed, popped in a load of laundry, and made sure they were showered and ready for a repeat of the same tomorrow. Frank got up from his chair only to say goodnight to the kids and make sure they were tucked in. On his way back to the living room, he grabbed a snack, plopped back in his chair, and turned on the television. Exhausted, Stella joined him.

Now 11:00, they were both ready for bed. Lying next to each other, Frank was feeling a bit frisky tonight. He reached for his wife, hoping to ignite her interest. Stella just lay there. So Frank became a little more aggressive and began rubbing her back. Married for nearly twelve years now, Stella knew his pattern when he wanted to make love. The problem was that she was not interested tonight, so she continued to just lie there, hoping Frank would possibly surmise that she had already fallen asleep. Not to be denied, Frank stepped it up one more notch and started kissing her neck as he unromantically queried through stale coffee breath, "Hey, wanna do it tonight?"

Stella, between a rock and a hard place, knew that if she declined, then Frank would roll over with an indignant *humph* and lie stewing next to her. But if she gave in, as she so often did, then she would be the one resenting her husband and feel like she sent the message that his evening's behavior was deserving of their bedtime rendezvous. Sound familiar?

Stereotypes suggest that guys tend to want sex all the time, wherever and whenever they think about it. Women, on the other hand, are much more methodical and need to be romanced. I think the following account spells it out pretty clearly:

Two married buddies were out drinking one night when one turned to the other and said, "You know, I don't know what else to do. Whenever I go home after we've been out drinking, I turn the headlights off before I get to the drive-way, shut off the engine, and coast into the garage. I take my shoes off before I go into the house, I sneak up the stairs, and I get undressed in the bathroom. I ease into bed and my wife still wakes up and yells at me for staying out so late!"

His buddy looked at him and said, "Well, you're obviously taking the wrong approach. I screech into the driveway, slam the door, storm up the steps, throw my shoes into the closet, jump into bed, slap her on the butt, and say, 'You as horny as I am?'...and she always acts like she's sound asleep!"[67]

For women, timing, mood, and atmosphere become much more important than carrying out the act itself. Gary Smalley says it best, "Men are like microwaves. Women are like crock pots."[68] Recognizing her prerequisite need for affection and romance, we can become more sensitive to her desire for intimacy in the bedroom. It's not that married women lose their desire for sex; it's that most husbands don't know how to stimulate and nurture that passion or simply lose the patience and resolve to do so. Married women have said:

- "I enjoy sex when we have it. But if I never had to do it again, no loss."

- "After straightening the house, cooking and cleaning up dishes, bathing and putting kids to bed, making love becomes just another chore on my to-do list."

- "He just expects it. He makes no effort to romance me."

As men we have the unparalleled privilege of setting the bedroom tone. If you make it your habit to court her during the day and remove some responsibilities and stresses from her, she may have a heightened desire in the evening. If you communicate your interest to make love to her earlier in the day, it gives her a chance to emotionally and physically prepare herself. But whether or not the evening culminates in wild, passionate sex or even casual, relaxed sex, enjoy your wife and be sweet to her all day because she's your wife. When you turn on the charm simply because you want sex, that's known as manipulation, and your wife will resent it.

For you ice-cream lovers, think of enjoying a big ice-cream sundae made with your favorite flavors and then covered with your choice of the finest toppings. Capping it off is a generous serving of whipped cream along with nuts and sprinkles. Any combination goes, and you can have as much or as little as you prefer. The final decorative touch is the optional cherry. Now a masterpiece, the sundae is everything you would want it to be, ready for your ultimate delight and consumption. You can devour it quickly or savor each spoonful. Either way you will enjoy it because it was constructed to your specifications with your approval in mind. Whether or not the optional cherry made its appearance will hardly have an effect on your overall experience to enjoy this delectable dessert.

Sex is the optional cherry. Your love for your wife and commitment to your relationship should be intact whether or not sex makes the lineup for that evening. You can derive pleasure from so many other irreplaceable qualities about her. Like the ice–cream sundae, enjoy the whole dessert without obsessing over one optional ingredient. Your sexual gratification is certainly important, but don't lose sight of the bigger picture. The more you can appreciate everything else about her, then sex becomes the added bonus.

In counseling we are often asked the ubiquitous question "What's the average number of times for a couple to have sex each week?" I guess we could poll thousands of couples and compute an average number, but that still would not accurately reflect the norm for this response. What works well for one couple may be completely different for another. Whether you make love to your spouse once a day or once a month is not a predictor of what other couples are doing. And if you've been married for any length of time, you know that seasons change depending on what's going on in your life.

Interestingly, women respond very differently to outside stress and stimuli. Some women make love after they've resolved a conflict to prove their truce; others don't. Some women make love to receive comfort during a time of grief; others wouldn't think of it. Only you will know what makes your wife tick and how to respond to her.

You need to collaboratively determine what each other needs and desires sexually and find a way to talk about it. Open communication may be uncomfortable at first, but it is essential if you are to take any strides forward. When it comes to lovemaking, ask each other:

- What turns you on?

- What turns you off?

- What do you enjoy?

- What makes you feel uncomfortable?

- Do you have any hang–ups I should know about?

- Anything else I need to know?

If you make it all about her, and not about yourself, then you're on your way to a triumphant solution. Your wife is your greatest treasure, and making love to her should always be a privilege for you, not an obligation or expectation.

IS ARGUING HEALTHY?

"A happy marriage is the union of two good forgivers."

Ruth Bell Graham

After twenty–plus years of marriage, she wants a divorce. He asks, "I think you owe me a solid reason. I worked my tail off for you and the kids to have a nice life, and you owe me a reason that makes sense. I want to hear it," to which she responds, "Because when I watch you eat…When I see you asleep…When I look at you lately, I just want to smash your face in."[69]

The above quote comes from the movie "The War of the Roses" but is sadly representative of many relationships. What started out with so much promise has now crashed upon the rocks of hopelessness. You've heard it said that "…there is a fine line between love and hate." The same person who just whispered "I love you" hours earlier is now spewing words of hatred and disgust. "How can this be?" you ask. Welcome to the fragile nature of marriage.

Some say that arguing within a marriage is healthy. Furthermore, if you don't argue, you are suppressing your true feelings, and those bottled–up emotions can cause a volatile explosion at some future point. While that may make a certain amount of sense at face value, and I concur that you will have disagreements that need to be met head–on—let me spin it another way. It is an interesting phenomenon that we can be polite and considerate to strangers and yet behave cruelly to our partners, whom we are supposed to love. The reality is that closer relationships present more opportunities for conflicts to surface than casual acquaintances do.

There are certain relationships in life that I would never disgrace by losing my temper or spiraling crazily out of control. For instance, I would never have a shouting match with my minister if I did not fully agree with Sunday morning's sermon. I would not dare scream at the judge in an open courtroom if I didn't like his ruling. When my child's teacher does something that I question, I schedule a meeting and have a civil sit–down discussion; I don't get in her face and threaten her within an inch of her life. When I don't see eye to eye with the boss on a company decision or policy, I don't go postal on him right there in the office. These are examples of individuals who play an important role in my life and hold a place of some authority. When addressing those persons, I treat them with the respect and restraint they deserve or that they have earned by the position they hold, regardless of whether or not I agree with them.

Why should it be anything less for your wife? She, too, is a person of significance in your life. She plays the principal role and deserves respect simply because of the position she holds within the family—as your wife and likely the mother of your children. Then what gives you the right to scream and curse and demean her because you disagree about something?

Many married people say that it's healthy to argue things out and then resolve the conflict. And for the most part, I concur. Yet I am concerned about the rules of engagement employed surrounding said conflict and resolution. Fights lead to saying mean–spirited things and feelings getting hurt. Offended mates then withdraw, and the relationship is left unsettled. It's no wonder some homes are colder than ice–skating rinks with husbands and wives always at odds with one another. If marriages are going to survive the inevitable battles that arise, I think we need to take a closer look at our strategies for handling those challenges.

Ann Landers said, "All married couples should learn the art of battle as they should learn the art of making love. Good battle is objective and honest—never vicious or cruel. Good battle is healthy and constructive, and brings to a marriage the principle of equal partnership."[70]

So is arguing healthy? If you did not argue within marriage, would the converse be true—that your marriage is unhealthy? For the record, there is no such thing as a conflict–free marriage. Recognize that you will disagree on some issues. No matter how much of a saint you might be, it is inescapable that you will have disagreements with your spouse. People are as different as the day is long. Because your wife is not your clone, your opinions will sometimes differ—and that's a good thing. Better to know in advance that conflict will arise. Your ability to deal with and resolve those disputes will not only determine the peace barometer of your household but is also predictive of how healthy a marriage relationship you will continue to have.

"Differentiate between solvable and unsolvable matters, and leave the unsolvable ones alone."

Differentiate between solvable and unsolvable matters, and leave the unsolvable ones alone. You may simply have to agree to disagree. And on minor matters that is okay. Don't allow contempt, disrespect, or hatred to furtively pop up like weeds in a newly seeded flowerbed. Accept one another's contrary opinions on matters you can live with. Bigger issues that cause contention may require some outside intervention. So if you are going to "go at it" with one another, at least have resolution as part of your objective. Before you blindly proceed, it is important to recognize some of the critical components necessary to successfully resolve differences within your marriage.

Initiate Resolution

So many disagreements could be rectified if we could get over ourselves and be the first to say sorry. Even if the other person is clearly in the wrong, you could still apologize for your insensitivity, or for causing them to freak out, or for not fully understanding what they were feeling or saying. A peace–seeking person is someone who is willing to lay down their pride and take positive measures to restore their relationship without making the other person feel guilty or making yourself look good. Conflict stalemates are the worst relationship killers. The longer a matter goes unaddressed and, therefore, unresolved, the greater the risk of emotional detachment you may incur.

Human nature needs to vent. If we're not connecting with our mate to release this pressure, then we open ourselves up to complaining about her to someone else. That's called gossip. Or we place her in the pickle of needing to discuss our problems with a girlfriend or her mother because we are unwilling to deal with it. Recognize the problem and be proactive to talk it out.

Pick the Right Place and Time

At a social event we connected with a certain couple and had agreed that we should all get together. Well, true to our word, we invited them over and they accepted. They arrived without any children so they could enjoy some "adult time." Since the venue was our house, our children were home and busily playing upstairs, at that time the oldest being seven years old.

We were enjoying our kitchen conversation and getting to know one another when, all of a sudden, something said triggered the wife. She flew off the handle and started flinging accusations at her husband. "You don't care about me. You're so selfish. All you do is think about your own agenda." Now if this was in a normal tone, it would have been uncomfortable enough. But imagine this…We are sitting around a four–seat kitchenette table. Her chair was thrown back from the table. She was wagging her finger right in her husband's face. And her rage was piqued so that she was screaming at the top of her lungs. The husband was squirming in his seat, denying the allegations, obviously humiliated by his wife's display of unabashed openness in front of what was intended to be their newfound friends.

After absorbing the shock of it all, my first thought was to shelter my children and buffer them from this barrage of insults. Running upstairs, I checked on them while tucking them away in a back bedroom, but there was frankly no way to screen them from this tumultuous outburst in our modest two–story home.

As inconspicuously as possible, Janet and I cast each other sideways glances, attempting to see which one of us had a clue what to do next or how to bring resolve to this out–of–control dilemma. Janet's eyes were bugging out as she continued kicking me under the table, desperate for me to bring the situation back under control.

Then and there I learned a life lesson regarding conflict resolution. Unloading at our house that night was not the best timing, nor was it the right venue for this couple to work out their differences. Find the proper time and setting to have mature, even heated discussions to resolve differences. Make sure the mood is right and you are both ready for the confrontation. Ask, "Do you have a few minutes to talk about something that is really bothering me?" This more gentle and respectful approach gives your mate some lead time to prepare her head and heart.

If matters heat up too much, then take a break. That's not to say you can childishly huff out of the room and slam doors or leave the house for the night. But it's okay to say, "Hey, can we take a time–out? My head is spinning and I'm afraid that I'll say something I might regret." Later, when your temper has cooled down, talk civilly and ask how you might resolve this.

Don't Let Things Add Up

Address a matter with your wife as soon as you feel the negativity rising within you. If at all possible, try to resolve it the day it happens. That's not to say that you shouldn't try to internally work some issues out on your own. But don't wait until you are fuming and about to blow your stack. The longer you let things stew, the harder it will be to resolve. And when you address it, stick to the topic at hand. Couples tend to start fighting over a specific topic and then dredge up every single thing that has ever made them mad.

To say that moving from New York to Georgia was a culture shock would be an understatement in many ways. But one of the more obvious advantages is the milder winters. No longer did I have to scrape ice off windshields and shovel driveways to start my day off to work. Snow became a distant memory in this foreign Southern land. It was actually pretty amusing because whenever a newscaster would even mention the slight possibility of an overnight snow dusting, the locals would madly rush to the supermarkets and empty the shelves of milk, bread, toilet tissue, and other staples.

On the rare occasion that it did snow, I would bundle the kids up and we would all go out in the front yard to take a crack at making a snowman. Janet would sometimes join us, but often she was more satisfied to watch from her cozy vantage point at the front window, ready to dry off the kids, serve hot chocolate, and warm them up on a moment's notice.

We began our formation by creating a small snowball that we kept packing more snow upon until it became too large to hold. Then we placed that icy sphere on the ground and began to roll it forward so that other snow could adhere to its wet surface and continue to build upon it. As the snowball grew, we lined up next to each other and helped push it around the front yard, leaving a trail of exposed grass in our wake. The accumulation of all that snow rolled up into a giant oversized ball would then become one of the tiers for our snowman.

When marriages have some unresolved issues at the foundation, it's as if the starting snowball is already formed. And then other problems add to the mass, and the accumulation causes the conflict to enlarge. It's as if you were rolling that snowball around the yard and then pushed it over the side of a hill. Momentum—even without additional interference—causes it to get bigger and bigger and roll faster and faster. Don't ever let your marital differences get to the point where the gravity and acceleration of your conflict overtakes your ability to keep things under control. Deal with issues as they arise rather than storing them as ammunition for future disputes.

Set Parameters

When two fighters enter the boxing ring, although they are prepared to beat each other's brains out, they agree to certain predetermined rules so that the end result can be determined fairly. In this case of boxing:

- Use a mouthpiece.

- No punching below the belt.

- No head butting.

- Don't strike your opponent while they are down.

While I'm not certain that comparing the sport of boxing to marital strife is the best analogy, the point I'm trying to make is that you and your wife should adhere to some guidelines—whether previously discussed or not—when working through disagreements within your marriage.

It is highly unlikely that you both will sit down together and review the game plan for arguing, like some football coach drawing X's and O's on the chalkboard. Experience and reconciliation will teach you that there are certain pitfalls to avoid when immersed in these trying moments. At calmer times you may even want to discuss some mistakes of past arguments so that you can improve your chance for more effective and expedient resolve next time around.

Some ground rules are obvious. Never raise your hand to your wife. It is cowardly as well as illegal! Beyond that, you are not your wife's keeper. You don't have to train her. You don't have to correct her. You don't have to shame her. You have to partner with her. So if you would not walk into work and slap your female boss in the face or curse out your female colleague or insult the woman in the next cubicle, then why would you behave so barbarically at home?

Never threaten her security—whether it be her physical safety, financial support, or by divorce. That's manipulation, and it's dirty play. It is up to the two of you to establish some clear boundaries and not ever compromise those parameters.

Don't accuse by using the word "you." Instead, take responsibility for your own feelings and actions by using the word "I." Listen to the subtle difference in these two statements: 1) "You never listen to me!" 2) "I feel like you don't listen to me when I talk." The first is accusatory and inflammatory; the second accepts responsibility for feeling a certain way without blaming the other person. Practice this strategy and save your marriage from any unnecessary verbal fisticuffs.

For us, we have sworn never to use the "D" word—divorce. It reminds me of the couple who had been married for forty–five years, had raised a brood of eleven children, and were blessed with twenty–two grandchildren. When asked the secret for staying together all that time, the wife said, "Many years ago we made a promise to each other: the first one to pack up and leave has to take all the kids."[71]

Just because things get tough or you want your way, that is not justification for threatening your marriage with failure. What security would my wife have if every time we "got into it" I said something impulsively stupid to threaten divorce? Janet and I made an early pledge to one another. We vowed that we would never intimidate the other with divorce, regardless of the severity of the disagreement or the extent of our frustration. Simply don't make it an option. If you do not make divorce an alternative for you, then subconsciously you will realize that you are bonded to this person, even stuck with her, for a lifetime. By understanding your commitment, you will be forced to compromise, negotiate, and find solutions for your challenges.

Be Careful What You Say

When you say something hurtful to your bride, it is like plucking a feather from a chicken. Each further derogative remark symbolizes plucking additional feathers from that chicken. Once you have said all the cruel and cutting things you could think of—or plucked all the feathers from the chicken—the damage is done. An apology will not mend your wife's wounded spirit any more than you will be able to put those loose feathers back into the chicken. It would be like throwing those feathers in the wind and then trying to gather them again.

Remember the old children's rhyme "sticks and stones may break my bones, but names will never harm me"? That's about as untrue as the Pope not being Catholic. Words sting and will be remembered long after the altercation is over. In nature, when a relatively docile animal is cornered by a predator, its fangs and claws come out as a defensive mechanism. It may even snarl, hiss, or spit to let its attacker know there will be a price to pay for this encounter. So it is in some marital sparring. When you corner your wife and make her feel vulnerable, you are stripping her of her protective covering and causing her to unload on you as well. Be careful of the buttons you push, because each has a set reaction and an ultimate cost.

There is never a good reason to belittle your wife when addressing something that might have set you off. You should both be able to express yourselves without fear of the other walking out the door. Don't call names, place blame, or drag the kids into your argument. There will be no winners in that case—only harm that will be difficult to undo.

Victor and Carol were married for more than twenty years. To everyone, their union seemed like a match made in heaven. They always seemed so peaceful and affectionate toward one another. Little did we know that a storm was brewing within Victor. Through a sequence of unfortunate events, Victor's infidelities were exposed, and like a cornered animal he fought back, spewing a tirade of accusations at Carol and justifications for his own behavior. Unfortunately, his teen daughter was in the room and heard Victor scream at her mom, "I never wanted these kids in the first place. You were the one who wanted them and thought it would help our marriage." Although the couple's anger has long since blown over, his comments are now engraved on his daughter's mind forever.

When a matter spirals out of control, rational behavior is often thrown aside. Again, if you feel like you're headed toward saying something you will regret, take a break. Go blow off some steam. Return only when you are both ready to resume civilly for the purpose of an amicable resolution.

Especially, don't drag up the past. Pulling out old hurts and infractions will only escalate a matter. Don't keep a record of wrongs like a teacher with a grading book. Even if you seem to revisit the same disagreement, that is not reason to bring up your past grievances. Let bygones be bygones.

Actively Listen

Ignoring or stonewalling your wife when she tries to initiate a discussion about a problem will only make matters worse. This can be very destructive to a relationship because it signals that you are not interested in resolving your difference or perhaps you are giving up altogether.

There have been occasions over the years where I've had to confront one of my children regarding misbehavior. I would sit the offender in front of me and begin my well–prepared lecture with all the inflections and combined delivery of a courtroom litigator turned motivational speaker. The accused would sit motionless, eyes glazed over, quietly awaiting my thunderous closing. Were they listening well? Or had they traveled to the recesses of their imagination to a happier place in order to endure my droning?

When listening to your wife's side concerning a disagreement, don't mentally check out. Nothing is more frustrating to her than the feeling that she is not being heard. Affirm her and make sure she knows that you clearly hear what she is trying to convey whether or not you agree with it. She must know that you are listening and care about what she has to say.

Yolanda did not want Joey to go back to his old job at the union. Although they were strapped for cash trying to run their own business, she was adamant about him not taking on any extra work. Joey felt like she was playing head games with him and that he couldn't please her no matter what. Out of one side of her mouth she was whining over their insufficient finances, yet when he showed his willingness to step up and work a second job, Yolanda seemed ungrateful and unsupportive. He just didn't get her. What she failed to clearly convey was that she did not like the influences the old job had on him. Hanging out with his work buddies and frequently working out–of–town projects made her feel totally insecure. Yolanda clearly recalled how his past improprieties had hurt their relationship and did not want to travel that route again. However, she did not want to air her distrust and risk a big blowup. She simply felt more comfortable having him around trying to work harder at their present business together.

In listening, you may sometimes have to hear more than just her words. You may have to hear her heart. Your wife will have valuable insight. Be open to her influence. Listen to her opinions and feelings, and let those opinions and feelings influence how you think and the decisions you make.

Admit It When You Are Wrong
(Don't gloat when you're right.)

Let's face it, guys, over the course of a relationship there will be times you are right and times you will be wrong. Yes, I said it...There will be times when it will be your fault. Sometimes you will just have to suck it up and admit your imperfections or idiocy. Be willing to acknowledge when you have made mistakes.

The question has been raised: Why did it take Moses forty years to cross the wilderness when it should have been less than a two–week journey? The answer: Like most men, he simply refused to stop and ask for directions.[72]

If you insist on being right all the time, then you are setting your marriage up for disaster. It is easy to become defensive and blame your spouse for something while denying any responsibility yourself or making excuses for a mistake. It's not about who's right or wrong. Of course there are two sides to every story. Some say there are three sides—his, hers, and the truth somewhere in the middle. Take a look at how you each contribute to the problem. The point is to find a resolution both of you can be comfortable with.

Through the years we have taught our children about not being sore losers, but to lose with decorum and be sure to congratulate the opponent. We have also trained them not to be sore winners, rather to handle themselves with poise and humility while allowing the other team to maintain their dignity in spite of defeat. Being right or being wrong within the context of marriage is not exactly about winning or losing. It is about exercising tact and embracing a partnership mentality, because after the encounter, the two of you still have to play house together. Would you rather be right or happily married?

Brainstorm possible solutions. Agree on a solution to try.

Each of you needs to share some recommended solutions. Negotiation and compromise are key. Try something you both agree on and see if it works. If unsuccessful, try something different next time around.

David and Joanne were having problems disciplining their nine-year-old daughter. She didn't want to do her chores. Whenever Joanne stepped up to deal with it, David would interfere and tell her she was overreacting. Not only was this causing tremendous conflict in their marriage, but their daughter was getting away with highway robbery as she played one parent against the other. When David and Joanne came to our office, they were completely exasperated. We asked them to begin thinking about some suggestions on how this could be handled as we helped facilitate the process. After an interactive brainstorming session, they came up with an agreeable solution. David and Joanne agreed to discuss what chores were absolutely necessary for their daughter to handle. They then sat down with their daughter and charted out a reward system, allotting points for each of her completed chores. If she failed to carry out a chore, she would lose points. When she attained a certain number of overall points, she would be rewarded by being allowed specific privileges that had all been previously agreed upon. Now instead of having an explosive home front, the daughter could hardly wait to fulfill her chores. Conflict resolved!

Never Go to Bed Angry

This seems so elementary, but let me tell you firsthand what a challenge it can be. Bedtime is that final frontier when kids are asleep, responsibilities have been set aside, and the house is quiet. It is very tempting to use this private setting to address marital problems. With both of you lying together, heads on pillows, staring at the ceiling, the mind races rehearsing the day's events.

One way to avoid bedtime ire is to simply agree not bring up the day's squabbles as pillow talk once you hit the sack. Personally, I don't like dealing with the world's problems in bed and making an adversary out of my wife. Whatever differences you may have dealt with prior to bedtime, choose to make peace or at least call a time–out. Whether or not you are at fault, your involvement still represents an offense to your wife. So make it right.

A couple was celebrating their golden wedding anniversary on the beaches of Montego Bay, Jamaica. Their domestic tranquility had long been the talk of the town. People would say, "What a peaceful and loving couple." The local newspaper reporter was inquiring as to the secret of their long and happy marriage.

The husband replied: "Well, it dates back to our honeymoon in America," explained the man. "We visited the Grand Canyon, in Arizona, and took a trip down to the bottom of the canyon by horse. We hadn't gone too far when my wife's horse stumbled and she almost fell off. My wife looked down at the horse and quietly said, 'That's once.' We proceeded a little farther and her horse stumbled again. Once more my wife quietly said, 'That's twice.' We hadn't gone a half mile when the horse stumbled for the third time. My wife quietly whispered, 'That's three.' She removed a revolver from her purse and shot the horse dead.

"I shouted at her, 'What's wrong with you, woman! Why did you shoot the poor animal like that? Are you crazy?' She looked at me and quietly said, 'That's once.' And from that moment on…we have lived happily every after."[73]

Tomorrow is another day. If you are still bothered by an issue, other opportunities will present themselves for discussion. In his fable of *The Town Mouse and the Country Mouse*, Aesop stated, "A crust eaten in peace is better than a banquet partaken in anxiety."[74] Do whatever it takes to restore peace. Be the initiator. Forgive and ask forgiveness.

Let Love Be Your Motivator

Whenever you are trying to resolve a matter, it is so important that your motivation be honorable and rightly placed. Are you looking to restore peace to your marriage? Or did you want to prove that you were right all along? Are you hoping to truly resolve a conflict? Or did you want to hang your partner out to dry because she was wrong? If we can take a moment to introspect as we engage in conflict–resolution measures, be sure to assess your intentions. Focus on the greater good. It is more important to safeguard the dignity of your relationship than it is to be right. Successful resolutions result in a deeper relationship. Do all things out of love—even when you don't feel it.

Some will tell you that the best part of any argument is making up. It may result in further intimacy because it shows both of you that you can disagree yet find a way to compromise and still love each other. For John and Julia, they punctuate their reconciliation by making wild, uninhibited love, proving to one another that everything is okay between them. (This could almost make it tempting to pick a fight just so you can make up!) For Dillon and Laura, after a resolved argument they each require some intentional space from one another in order to reflect on the matter and heal from the verbal and emotional exchange. The last thing on their minds would be intimacy. You'll discover through your own experiences how the aftermath of conflict resolution works in your household. It may even help you determine which battles are worth fighting and which are better left alone. At the least, respect each other's differences of opinion and use these times to grow closer to one another.

ROME WAS NOT BUILT IN A DAY

"For two people in a marriage to live together day after day is unquestionably the one miracle the Vatican has overlooked."

Bill Cosby

For many of us, our marriages may not be exactly where we want them, but we don't have to resign ourselves to that being our final fate. Within our power is the ability to swing the pendulum in the completely opposite arc if we would only be willing to take the appropriate tactical measures toward success. If you want a strong financial portfolio, then one must make the right deposits and investments to ensure that wealth. The same is true with marriage. If you want a great marriage, make deposits of trust, kindness, compliments, and romance. Invest in learning, listening, communicating, and protecting her at all costs. You can have a completely fulfilling marital relationship by taking charge of what lies within your ability to control.

Don't sweat the small stuff. I remember one particular evening when we invited our friends over along with their two children. Their kids were the same ages as our two older children, so it was a perfect match. The kids all preoccupied each other so that the parents could visit. The adults were sitting around the kitchen table playing a card game, telling stories, laughing, and noshing on snacks. Judy began to tell us about something that happened to a neighbor of theirs. As she was setting the stage, her husband, Paul, blindsided her.

"No, dear. It was not on a Monday. It was a Tuesday."

Taken back by his interruption, she held her ground and said, "I'm pretty certain it happened on Monday. Anyway…" and she attempted to resume her narration, to which Paul again interjected, "No. It was Tuesday. I'm sure of it."

This went on a couple more times. And all the while the day on which the event occurred was irrelevant to the story line. It did not matter whatsoever, not in the least.

The funny thing is the indelible imprint it made in my mind all these years later, and I still have no clue what that story was about. It was just idle chitchat amongst a group of friends. But Janet and I clearly remember how Paul rudely broke into Judy's story to correct her in front of us regarding a minor point that added no value to the story. Unfortunately for him, Paul's rude and demeaning tone toward his wife is what has stood the test of time in our memory banks.

There are so many thoughtless things we do on a daily basis that can sabotage our relationship. Become a student of your marriage and practice what works while avoiding what does not. We all know what puts a smile on our partner's face and what can cause devastating damage. Choose the former.

"The condition of your marriage is a direct result of what you have put into it thus far."

As we wrap up, let me remind you that the condition of your marriage is a direct result of what you have put into it thus far. None of us like to accept that awesome sense of responsibility slapped on us, especially if our marriage is presently somewhat anemic. The easiest thing to do would be to blame that no–good partner of yours for not carrying her fair share in trying to make the relationship work. Keep in mind that not every lackluster relationship means that the partners don't care and are not trying. You just may have been trying the wrong things. Or you may have had so many disappointments along the way that it's become easier to stop trying altogether. It is my sincere hope that you embrace the concepts detailed in this book and apply them to your marriage with renewed hope.

You would do well to remember the following initiatives in order to set them in motion within your relationship. Each of these has already been discussed at length.

- Cherish her by how you speak and act toward her.

- Remember that it's not your responsibility to try to change your partner but to love her where she is.

- Never stop growing and learning how to be a better husband.

- Treat her like royalty.

- Prefer her above all else.

- Be a one–woman man.

- Trust is priceless and should not be easily forfeited.

- Protect her at all costs: physically, emotionally, relationally, and financially.

- Let her into your heart by talking to her and sharing your feelings.

- Brag on her publicly as well as privately. Compliments yield high dividends.

- Let her vent without risk of reprisal or repercussions.

- Look the best you can look. Take care of your health.

- Let her know she is your number–one priority by always making time for her.

- Keep romance alive in your marriage.

- Make sure lovemaking is all about her.

- Never use the "d" word—divorce—so that it doesn't become an option.

- Exceed her expectations of you while placing no expectations on her.

- Love her your best. Don't leave any regrets on the table.

Finally, enjoy life and grow old gracefully together. I heard the story about a concerned husband who went to the doctor to talk about his wife.

"Doctor, I think my wife is deaf because she never hears me the first time and always asks me to repeat things."

"Well," the doctor replied, "go home and tonight, stand about fifteen feet from her, and say something to her. If she doesn't reply, move about five feet closer and say it again. Keep doing this so that we'll get an idea about the severity of her deafness."

Sure enough, the husband went home and did exactly as instructed. He started off about fifteen feet from his wife in the kitchen as she was chopping some vegetables and said, "Honey, what's for dinner?" He heard no response. So he moved about five feet closer and asked again. No reply. He moved another five feet closer. Still no reply. He got fed up and moved right behind her, about an inch away, and asked again, "Honey, what's for dinner?"

She replied, "For the fourth time, vegetable stew!"[75]

Marriage can and should be an awesome experience. Certainly it takes managing, negotiating, sharing, and sometimes even denying yourself, but the benefits so outweigh any perceived sacrifices. Rather than putting up your guard, throw caution to the wind and love her your best. If in doing so, things still don't work out for reasons beyond your control, you will have complete peace of mind without any regrets. To love and be loved by someone for a lifetime is the ultimate gift.

BIBLIOGRAPHY

Arthur, Kay. *A Marriage without Regrets.* Eugene: Harvest House Publishers, 2000.

Chapman, Dr. Gary. *The Five Love Languages.*

Gray, Ph.D., John. *Men Are From Mars, Women Are From Venus.* New York: HarperCollins Publishers, 1992.

Harley, Jr., Willard F. *Fall In Love, Stay In Love.* Grand Rapids: Baker Book House, 2001.

LaHaye, Tim. *I Love You, but Why Are We so Different?* Eugene: Harvest House Publishers, 1991.

McGraw, Dr. Phil. *Love Smart.* New York: Free Press, 2005.

Morley, Patrick M. *What Husbands Wish Their Wives Knew about Men.* Grand Rapids: Zondervan, 1998.

Olson, David H. and Amy K. Olson. *Empowering Couples: Building On Your Strengths.* Second Edition. Minneapolis: Life Innovations, Inc., 2000.

Parrott, Drs. Les and Leslie. *Love Is...* Grand Rapids: Zondervan, 1999.

Parrott, Drs. Les & Leslie. *Saving Your Marriage Before It Starts.* Grand Rapids: Zondervan, 1995.

Schlessinger, Dr. Laura. *The Proper Care & Feeding of Marriage.* New York: HarperCollins Publishers, 2007.

Smalley, Gary. *Making Love Last Forever.* Dallas: Word Publishing, 1996.

Smalley, Dr. Gary. *The DNA of Relationships.* Colorado Springs: Smalley Publishing Group LLC, 2004.

Smalley, Gary. *The Marriage You've Always Dreamed Of.* Colorado Springs: Smalley Publishing Group LLC, 2005.

Smith, Robin L. *Lies at the Altar: The Truth about Great Marriages.* New York: Hyperion, 2006.

Waite, Linda J. & Gallagher, Maggie. *The Case for Marriage.* New York: Doubleday, 2000.

ENDNOTES

What Is Love?

1. Merriam–Webster's Online Dictionary

2. Helen Steiner Rice. *The Magic of Love.*

3. 1 Corinthians 13:5–7, NIV

4. Gettysburg Address, http://www.gettysburgaddress.com/HTMLS/ga.html

5. United States Constitution, Preamble, http://www.usconstitution.net/xconst_preamble.html

6. *Twelve Days of Christmas*, http://www.carols.org.uk/the_twelve_days_of_christmas.htm

7. http://answers.yahoo.com/question/

8. http://www.webcontent.com/articles/153/1/Online–Dating–Statistics/Page1.html

9. http://www.onlinedatingmagazine.com/mediacenter/onlinedatingfacts.html

10. Henny Youngman, http://thinkexist.com/quotes

11. http://marriage.rutgers.edu/

12. http://marriage–jokes.blogspot.com

13. Anonymous Author

14. http://marriage.about.com/cs/engagement/qt/reasons.htm

15. John Gray, Ph.D. *Men Are From Mars, Women Are From Venus.* Chapter 4: *How to Motivate the Opposite Sex*

Role Play

16. http://jokes4all.net

17. Based on a personal poll given to female friends and family members, both married and unmarried

18. http://www.jokesunlimited.com

19. http://www.weddingswithlove.net.au/humour.html

20. http://www.rd.com/housework–and–repair–jokes

21. http://www.butlerwebs.com/jokes/marriage3.htm

22. Dr. Seuss, http://www.wikipedia.org

Benefits of Marriage: The Delightful Dozen

23. Waite & Gallagher, 2000.

24. http://www.geocities.com/vertuosso/jokes.html

25. Waite & Gallagher, 2000.

26. Waite & Gallagher, 2000.

27. Waite & Gallagher, 2000.

28. http://findarticles.com/p/articles/mi_m1355/is_n1_v91/ai_18930297

29. Waite & Gallagher, 2000.

Finding Mrs. Right

30. Zig Ziglar, http://www.great–inspirational–quotes.com/marriage–quotes.html

31. *Last Holiday*, 2006, directed by Wayne Wang

32. "The Tonight Show with Jay Leno." *Popping the Magic Question.*

33. Dr. Robin L. Smith. *Lies at the Altar: The Truth about Great Marriages.*

34. *My Big Fat Greek Wedding*, 2002, Joel Zwick

35. http://www.verifine.org/Humor/jewish.html

Be a Student

36. Michael Jordan, http://www.wikipedia.org

37. Franz Joseph Haydn, http://www.wikipedia.org

38. J. Allan Petersen, http://christianlovestories.blog-spot.com/2007/03/marriage–is–empty–box.html

39. http://www.associatedcontent.com/article/35097/top_reasons_people_divorce.html

40. *Reader's Digest* survey, http://www.rd.com/content/ printContent.do?contentId=32011&KeepThis=true &TB_iframe=true&height=500&width=790&mod al=true

41. Fredrich Nietzsche, http://www.thinkexist.com

42. http://www.absolutelyjokes.com/ love–and–wedding/first–night

Put Her on a Pedestal

43. Traditional wedding vows, http://www.thewedding-network.com.au/weddingvows.htm

44. Dr. Gary Chapman. *The Five Love Languages.*

45. http://www.ahajokes.com

46. Presidential address, http://www.wikipedia.org

47. Og Mandino, http://www.quotes.net

48. http://www.freedomisknowledge.net

Make Her Feel Safe

49. http://www.abanet.org/domviol/statistics.html

50. http://www.funny.com

He Never Talks to Me…

51. As told to me by a friend.

52. http://nishflowers.com/florist_jokes.php

Compliment Her ... or Someone Else Will

53. http://www.rd.com/clean–jokes–and–laughs

54. http://marriagejokes.thejokeindex.com

55. Dr. Hook. "When You're In Love with a Beautiful Woman," http://www.lyricstime.com

56. Rupert Holmes. "Escape," (also called *The Piña Colada Song*) http://www.lyricsondemand.com/one-hitwonders/pinacoladalyrics.html

57. Johnny Lingo, http://www.ldsfilm.com/JohnnyLingo/JohnnyLingo.html

Kill Her with Kindness

58. *The Gift of the Magi*. O. Henry, 1906

59. Mark Twain, http://www.quotes.net/quote/1650

60. Proverbs 18:22, New Living Translation: "The man who finds a wife finds a treasure, and he receives favor from the Lord."

61. https://www.goofball.com/jokes/men_women

62. Ronald Reagan, http://quotations.about.com/od/weddingtoasts/a/wedding19.htm

He's Touching Me ...

63. "The Newlywed Game"

64. http://www.joking.sumpy.com/just–joking10.html

65. http://magnoliaheartbeats.blogspot.com

66. http://www.afunnystuff.com

67. http://forumgarden.com/forums/just–fun/1409–marraige–advice.html

68. Gary Smalley, as first heard in his video series, *Keys to Loving Relationships*, http://store.dnaofrelation-ships.com/index.asp?PageAction=VIEWPROD&ProdID=107

Is Arguing Healthy?

69. *The War of the Roses*, 1989, directed by Danny DeVito http://www.imdb.com/title/tt0098621/quotes

70. Ann Landers, http://www.quotationspage.com

71. http://www.tensionnot.com/jokes/wedding_jokes

72. As told to me by a friend.

73. https://www.liweddings.com/chat/topic–230424–1.html

74. Aesop's Fables. *The Town Mouse and the Country Mouse.*

Rome Was Not Built in a Day

75. http://www.basicjokes.com

listen|imagine|view|experience

AUDIO BOOK DOWNLOAD INCLUDED WITH THIS BOOK!

In your hands you hold a complete digital entertainment package. Besides purchasing the paper version of this book, this book includes a free download of the audio version of this book. Simply use the code listed below when visiting our website. Once downloaded to your computer, you can listen to the book through your computer's speakers, burn it to an audio CD or save the file to your portable music device (such as Apple's popular iPod) and listen on the go!

How to get your free audio book digital download:

1. Visit www.tatepublishing.com and click on the e|LIVE logo on the home page.
2. Enter the following coupon code:
    9c23-a223-d11a-fbf2-5bc4-4b79-4444-86f2
3. Download the audio book from your e|LIVE digital locker and begin enjoying your new digital entertainment package today!